BOUNTIFUL BOWLS

BOUNTIFUL BOWLS

FRESH, VIBRANT, AND NUTRITIOUS FLAVORS IN A BOWL

CONTENTS

THE POWER OF THE BOWL

THE POWER BOWL IS NOT A NEW PHENOMENON. MANY CULTURES HAVE MEAL-IN-A-BOWL TRADITIONS, RANGING FROM THE NORTHERN EUROPEAN BOWL OF OATMEAL TO THE KOREAN RICE DISH *BIBIMBAP*.

The recent growth in popularity of eating from a bowl has its roots in the early twenty-first century, with New York salad restaurant chains, such as Sweetgreen and Liquiteria, offering meals in a bowl as part of a mission to provide seasonal, healthy food in a fresh, appealing, no-nonsense way. Tuning in to the popular zeitgeist, and with a boost from food bloggers and social media, the bowl trend has made an impact on those who want a diet full of goodness. With their contents constantly being reinvented, bowls continue to make their way into our kitchens.

Simply put, food looks incredibly appetizing in a bowl. It has impact. It's certainly easy to eat—all you need is a fork and a variety of small or chopped ingredients that can be speared and chewed easily. Food in a bowl also provides flexibility. It's so simple to eat your meal informally—you can cradle a warming bowl in your hands as you talk with friends, or relax in the yard on a hot day with an easy salad bowl.

It's not just about the bowl. The power behind the bowl is that it can be filled with a healthy combination of colorful fruit and vegetables, lean protein, and great-tasting dressings, with a sprinkling of superfoods, such as shredded kale, grated carrot, alfalfa sprouts, or sunflower seeds, to round it off.

Power bowls, invariably full of color and bursting with healthy ingredients, are highly photogenic

(this is why they look so appetizing), and they have spread their allure on social media channels as people share their healthy and appetizing bowls on food blogs and platforms such as Twitter and Instagram.

Bowls break away from the predictable formula of recipes designed to serve four. That's fine if you are preparing a family meal, but what about if you live alone, want to eat at a different time, or just want to eat alone? Bowls let you escape from the traditional formulas of meals on a plate—ingredients are driven by fruit, vegetables, high protein content, and a rainbow of colors.

Power bowls are so named to explain the power punch of superfoods and nutrients that they offer, helping to keep you energized throughout the day. While there are no rules—you can use ingredients you really love to fit any cuisine or taste—there are certain types of bowls that have become popular.

Smoothie bowls are a delicious addition to the breakfast table and can also be served as a dessert. Examples here are the Summer Melon Bowl on page 26 or the Strawberry & Rhubarb Smoothie Bowl on page 164.

Breakfast bowls break away from the standard breakfast routine of cereal and milk, adding ingredients that will increase the nutritional value and the visual appeal of your first meal

of the day. Examples include both the Fruity Sweet Potato Breakfast Bowl on page 42 and Wake-Up Salad on page 44.

Buddha bowls, also referred to as sunshine or glory bowls, are named after oryoki, the traditional nested Buddha bowls used by Buddhist monks. These meatless meals for one are filling bowls of raw or roasted vegetables, beans, healthy grains, such as quinoa or brown rice, and plenty of greens. Toppings can include nuts or seeds and a drizzle of dressing. Why not try the Summer Abundance Salad on page 88 or the Harissa Veggie Bowl on page 112?

Poke bowls (pronounced "poh-keh"), meaning "slice and cut," are based on a traditional Hawaiian dish, which was originally just delicious raw fish and rice, similar to deconstructed sushi, seasoned to taste. They have now evolved to include cooked fish, salad ingredients, and seeds (see the Tuna Poke Bowl on page 72).

Bowls also offer a great choice for specific diets. Most of the bowls here cater for vegetarian, vegan, gluten-free, dairy-free, and raw diets and are identified with a key (see page 9). Examples include the Vegetable Rice Bowl on page 54, the Lentil & Amaranth Tabbouleh on page 124, and the Quinoa Fruit Salad on page 152.

Another attraction is the sheer simplicity of preparing a bowl. All the recipe bowls here are generally simple to put together. They use fresh ingredients that are chopped, grated, roasted, or blended, along with some that are cooked or steamed, to create great texture, with the addition of spices and herbs for flavor.

CREATING NUTRITIONAL BALANCE

The key to eating a balanced and nutritious diet is variety. We need basic micronutrients for optimum health—carbohydrates for energy, proteins for muscle repair and the immune system, and essential fats for brain and cell health. To help the body to break down the micronutrients, large amounts of macronutrients are needed—these are found in vitamins and minerals, and we get them principally from colorful fruits and vegetables. The traditional adage "eat a rainbow every day" steers people toward a daily intake of a variety of nutrients—and with bowl food, you can make sure you have a rainbow in every bowl.

BOWL INGREDIENTS

FRUIT AND VEGETABLES

We need to eat plenty of fruit and vegetables—half the plate (or bowl) of each meal or snack, most of which should be vegetables. Fruit and vegetables in different colors contain different vitamins, minerals, and phytochemicals, which all help to keep you healthy. Eat fruit and vegetables that are in season, and choose from local sources, if you can. You can chop, grate, roast, or steam vegetables and plan to make them at least 50 percent of your bowl. Avoid frying vegetables, because cooking at high temperatures can detrimentally affect the nutrients.

CEREALS, GRAINS, PASTA, RICE, NOODLES, AND POTATOES

Foods in this group provide energy and dietary fiber, a range of vitamins, minerals, and small amounts of protein. Choose whole-grain types, such as brown rice, whole-wheat pasta, and unrefined cereals, to keep your digestive system and heart healthy. Quinoa, brown rice, and noodles are all quick and nutritious and make a good base for other ingredients. These are great carbohydrate foods and are important for energy.

PROTEIN

Protein is essential for growth and the repair of cells. It also provides essential vitamins and minerals. It is wise to aim for 70–150 g (2½–5½ ounces) of protein with each meal. You can use fish, chicken, red meat, seafood, eggs, or cheese for your protein allowance. While dairy products are high in protein, nondairy milk, yogurt, and cheese, other than soy, have a low protein load. Vegetarians and vegans can combine grains and legumes, such as rice, quinoa, lentils, and beans, to get a full protein boost. Tofu works well with the addition of tasty spices and dressings.

HEALTHY UNSATURATED FATS

We need fat in our diet to help the body to absorb fat-soluble vitamins A, D, E, and K and to provide essential fatty acids. These are found in oily fish, such as salmon, mackerel, herring, and fresh tuna,

and in plant products, such as olive oil, flaxseed oil, avocados, pecans, and pumpkin seeds. When planning your bowl, aim to include about 10 percent healthy unsaturated fat.

HERBS

Herbs add great flavor to a wide range of dishes, and many have therapeutic qualities, too. Turmeric, for example, is a natural anti-inflammatory, mint helps aid digestion, and ginger also supports the digestive system.

Planning ahead will help you with your bowl preparation. Certain things can be made in bulk— dressings prepared in advance can be stored in the refrigerator, and chutneys and pickles made with fresh seasonal ingredients can be canned and stored until needed. Fruit purees can be frozen in ice cube trays. Other foods that can be made in advance include roasted vegetables, hummus, overnight oats, baked sweet potatoes, and coleslaw.

Whatever your food preferences, the power-bowl formula is a simple and dramatic way to serve up delicious food that is packed with nutrition.

KEY

GLUTEN-FREE · VEGETARIAN · DAIRY-FREE · RAW · VEGAN

The colored icons included with the recipes throughout the book indicate those that suit specific diets: vegetarian, gluten-free, dairy-free, raw, and vegan. This will be a useful guide if you follow any of these diets, or if you are preparing food for friends and family who follow a diet.

BREAKFAST

TURMERIC & CHIA OVERNIGHT OATS

TURMERIC HAS AN INGREDIENT CALLED CURCUMIN, A POWERFUL ANTI-INFLAMMATORY AND A STRONG ANTIOXIDANT, SO THIS BREAKFAST DISH IS A HEALTHY WAY TO START THE DAY.

10 mins, plus chilling | 5 mins | ②

INGREDIENTS

1¼ cups rolled oats

grated zest of 1 orange

1¾ cups fresh orange juice

¼ teaspoon ground turmeric

1 tablespoon chia seeds

⅔ cup hulled and sliced strawberries

¼ cup blueberries

½ cup raspberries

1 tablespoon pomegranate seeds

2 teaspoons dry unsweetened coconut

1. Put the oats into a medium saucepan.

2. Whisk together the orange zest, 1¼ cups of the orange juice, and the turmeric. Pour the mixture over the oats and cook, stirring, over low heat for 4–5 minutes.

3. Remove from the heat and stir in the remaining orange juice and the chia seeds. Divide between two bowls and chill in the refrigerator overnight.

4. When ready to serve, top each bowl with the strawberries, blueberries, raspberries, pomegranate seeds, and dry unsweetened coconut.

This recipe could also be served warm, topped with warming stewed fruits such as plums or rhubarb, with perhaps a dollop of plain yogurt.

PER SERVING : 399 CALS | 9.1G FAT | 2.6G SAT FAT | 73.1G CARBS | 24.6G SUGAR | 13G FIBER | 10.8G PROTEIN | TRACE SODIUM

COCONUT POWER BOWL

THIS RECIPE USES A DELICIOUS HOMEMADE QUINOA GRANOLA, WHICH IS RICHER IN PROTEIN AND LOWER IN SUGAR THAN MOST STORE-BOUGHT GRANOLAS.

INGREDIENTS

½ cup coconut oil

1 tablespoon honey

2 tablespoons packed dark brown sugar

1 cup quinoa flakes

1¾ cups rolled oats

3 tablespoons dry unsweetened coconut

½ teaspoon ground cinnamon

1 tablespoon dried cranberries

1 tablespoon chopped pecans

2 bananas, peeled and chopped

½ cup walnuts

¾ cup coconut milk

1 teaspoon ground cinnamon

¾ cup raspberries

¼ cup fresh mint leaves

2 tablespoons maple syrup

1. Preheat the oven to 350°F. Put the coconut oil, honey, and sugar into a saucepan over low heat and heat, stirring, until the sugar has dissolved.

2. Remove from the heat and stir in the quinoa flakes, ⅔ cup of the oats, 2 tablespoons of the dry unsweetened coconut, and the cinnamon, cranberries, and pecans. Mix well to combine.

3. Spread the mixture over a baking sheet and bake in the preheated oven for 15 minutes, stirring halfway through the cooking time.

4. Remove from the oven, spoon into a bowl, and let cool.

5. Meanwhile, put the bananas, remaining oats, the walnuts, and coconut milk into a food processor and process until almost smooth.

6. Pour into four bowls and add the granola. Top with the cinnamon, raspberries, mint, the remaining dry unsweetened coconut, and a drizzle of maple syrup.

PER SERVING : 43.1 CALS | 43.1G FAT | 26G SAT FAT | 84.7G CARBS | 31.3G SUGAR | 11.3G FIBER | 11.8G PROTEIN | 40MG SODIUM

BLUEBERRY OATMEAL PIE

HERE'S A DELICIOUS, FIBER-RICH BOWL OF OATMEAL PACKED WITH FRUIT AND FINISHED WITH A SWEET, STICKY, AND CRUNCHY TOPPING. EVERYONE WILL LOVE IT!

15 mins, plus soaking | None | 2

INGREDIENTS

1 cup raw rolled oats

1½ teaspoons chia seeds

2½ tablespoons raw dried coconut flakes

¾ teaspoon ground cinnamon

1 banana, peeled and coarsely chopped

juice of ¼ lemon

1¾ tablespoons raw honey

⅓ cup blueberries

1 cup raw coconut milk

2 tablespoons chopped raw almonds

½ tablespoon milled flaxseed

1 tablespoon sunflower seeds

1. Combine the oats, chia seeds, 2 tablespoons of the coconut flakes, and ½ teaspoon of the cinnamon in a mixing bowl.

2. Put the banana pieces into a small bowl. Sprinkle iwth the lemon juice and stir in 1 tablespoon of the honey, making sure each piece of banana is coated with the mixture. (You can warm the honey slightly if it's too solid to stir in.)

3. Stir the bananas, half the blueberries, and the coconut milk into the oat mixture and combine. Spoon evenly into two serving bowls, pressing the banana pieces into the oats. Cover the bowls with plastic wrap or foil and refrigerate overnight.

4. Meanwhile, start making the pie topping. In a small bowl, stir the almonds, flaxseed, and sunflower seeds together. Stir in the remaining cinnamon and honey, warmed if necessary. Mix thoroughly and let stand, covered, for the morning.

5. Before serving, sprinkle the topping over the oatmeal and decorate with the remaining coconut flakes and blueberries.

Although the oatmeal tastes great served cold, it can also be warmed gently to 104°F before you add the topping.

PER SERVING : 582 CALS | 29.6G FAT | 17.1G SAT FAT | 75G CARBS | 29.4G SUGAR | 14.6G FIBER | 12G PROTEIN | TRACE SODIUM

CREAMY RICOTTA BREAKFAST BOWL

A LIGHT, CREAMY BREAKFAST THAT IS PERFECT FOR A SUMMER MORNING.
TOP IT WITH SEASONAL FRUITS OF YOUR CHOICE.

INGREDIENTS

¾ cup ricotta cheese

grated zest of ½ orange

grated zest of 1 lemon

1 mango, peeled, pitted, and sliced

2 blood oranges, peeled and sliced

1 passion fruit, halved, flesh only

1 tablespoon gluten-free granola

1–2 teaspoons honey (optional)

1. Put the ricotta cheese into a medium bowl and stir through the grated orange zest and lemon zest.

2. Divide the mixture between two smaller bowls.

3. Top with the mango slices, blood orange slices, and passion fruit flesh, then sprinkle with the granola and honey, if using, and serve immediately.

You may want to omit the honey and sprinkle with ground cinnamon instead—this is a great way of adding flavor, and cinnamon is also known to help control blood-sugar levels.

PER SERVING : 369 CALS | 15.5G FAT | 8.7G SAT FAT | 38.6G CARBS | 23.8G SUGAR | 9.3G FIBER | 14.8G PROTEIN | 80MG SODIUM

ACAI & BERRY MORNING JAR

AFTER CHILLING THIS BREAKFAST JAR IN THE REFRIGERATOR OVERNIGHT, ALL YOU NEED TO DO IS ADD THE TOPPING FOR BREAKFAST—OR, INDEED, ANY MEAL OF THE DAY!

10 mins, plus resting and chilling

None

INGREDIENTS

⅔ cup hulled strawberries

¾ cup raspberries

¼ cup blueberries

⅔ cup raw coconut yogurt (see recipe below)

¼ cup raw coconut milk

½ teaspoon vanilla bean seeds

1 tablespoon chia seeds

2 teaspoons raw honey

1 teaspoon acai powder

½ tablespoon lemon juice

2 tablespoons raw cashew nut butter

1 teaspoon hemp seeds

2 fresh mint sprigs

RAW COCONUT YOGURT

1 cup fresh or frozen coconut meat, thawed if frozen

½ cup raw coconut water

1 probiotic powder capsule

1. To make the coconut yogurt, blend the coconut meat and coconut water in a blender until smooth. Empty the powder from the probiotic capsule into the mixture and blend again for a few seconds.

2. Pour the coconut mixture into a bowl, cover with plastic wrap or foil, and let stand in the kitchen overnight at warm room temperature. In the morning, you should have about 1¼ cups of yogurt. Remove what you need and the rest will keep in the refrigerator for up to a week.

3. Blend ½ cup of the strawberries, ½ cup of the raspberries, and 3 tablespoons of the blueberries with the yogurt, coconut milk, vanilla seeds, chia seeds, honey, acai powder and lemon juice until smooth. Pour the mixture into a wide-neck jar with a 12-fluid-ounce capacity. Cover and chill in the refrigerator overnight.

4. The following morning, top with the cashew butter and the remaining berries, followed by the hemp seeds and mint sprigs.

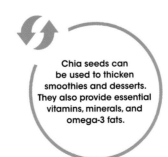

Chia seeds can be used to thicken smoothies and desserts. They also provide essential vitamins, minerals, and omega-3 fats.

PER SERVING : 897 CALS | 67.3G FAT | 42.7G SAT FAT | 72.1G CARBS | 34.6G SUGAR | 26.9G FIBER | 15.4G PROTEIN | 40MG SODIUM

PEAR, BANANA & APPLE BREAKFAST BOWL

IF YOU'RE TIRED OF EATING GRAINS FOR BREAKFAST, THIS FRUITY BREAKFAST BOWL WILL INVIGORATE—IT'S FULL OF FRESH AUTUMNAL FLAVORS, WARMING CINNAMON, AND DELICIOUS DRIED BERRIES.

15 mins, plus optional chilling

None

②

INGREDIENTS

2 ripe dessert pears, such as Bartlett

2 green-skinned apples, such as Granny Smith

1 large banana, peeled and chopped

⅓ cup apple juice

juice of ½ lemon

2 tablespoons golden raisins

2 tablespoons raw cashew nuts

1 tablespoon sunflower seeds

1 tablespoon raw sugar

½ teaspoon ground cinnamon

1 tablespoon golden berries

1 tablespoon cranberries

1. Core and chop one pear and one apple. Put them into a serving bowl with half the banana and pour half the apple juice and half the lemon juice over the fruit. Stir well to combine.

2. Core, peel, and coarsely chop the remaining pear and apple. Add them to a blender with the rest of the banana.

3. Add the remaining apple juice and lemon juice to the blender with the golden raisins and nuts. Blend until you have a finely chopped mixture.

4. Stir the blended mixture into the chopped fruit, along with the sunflower seeds, sugar, and cinnamon. Sprinkle with the golden berries and cranberries. Chill in the refrigerator if you have time, or serve immediately.

Golden berries are dried Cape gooseberries—the small and tangy orange fruits you can sometimes find for sale in winter.

PER SERVING : 438 CALS | 7.5G FAT | 1G SAT FAT | 93.8G CARBS | 62.5G SUGAR | 5.5G FIBER | 5.5G PROTEIN | TRACE SODIUM

VERY BERRY OVERNIGHT OATS

MADE IN A LIDDED JAR, THIS IS A PERFECT BREAKFAST TO BRING TO WORK. PREPARE YOUR OATS THE NIGHT BEFORE AND THEY'LL BE READY TO EAT OR PICK UP WITH NO FUSS IN THE MORNING.

15 mins, plus chilling · None · ①

INGREDIENTS

½ cup raw rolled oats

½ tablespoon milled flaxseed

½ tablespoon acai berry powder

2 teaspoons goji berries

1 tablespoon slivered almonds

½ tablespoon raw honey

½ cup almond milk

2 tablespoons blueberries

3 strawberries

1. Put the oats, flaxseed, acai berry powder, goji berries, most of the slivered almonds, the honey, and almond milk into a lidded jar with an 8-fluid-ounce capacity. Stir well.

2. Stir a few of the blueberries into the oat mixture. Seal the jar with the lid and chill in the refrigerator overnight.

3. In the morning, chop the strawberries. Top the oats with the remaining blueberries, strawberries, and the remaining almonds.

Acai berry powder is full of fiber, vitamin E, iron, and calcium, and is high in antioxidants.

PER SERVING : 437 CALS | 21.5G FAT | 1.7G SAT FAT | 52.3G CARBS | 15.9G SUGAR | 11.1G FIBER | 13.1G PROTEIN | TRACE SODIUM

SUMMER MELON BOWL

USING THE MELON AS A BOWL CREATES A UNIQUE CONTAINER FOR A DELICIOUSLY FRUITY START TO THE DAY, PACKED WITH THE TROPICAL TASTE OF COCONUT.

INGREDIENTS

1 cantaloupe, halved and seeds removed

1¼ cups raspberries

2 kiwis, cubed

⅓ cup coarsely chopped mint

juice of 1 lime

1 tablespoon coconut oil

¾ cup oats

¾ cup coconut yogurt, to serve

1. Using a large spoon, scoop the flesh from the melon, leaving the skin to create two melon "bowls." Cut the melon flesh into bite-size chunks and transfer half of the chunks into a large bowl, reserving the remainder for another meal. Add the raspberries, kiwis, chopped mint, and lime juice. Working carefully to avoid damaging the fruit, combine. Set aside.

2. Heat a small skillet over medium heat and add the coconut oil. Heat until melted before adding the oats and continue to cook for 3–4 minutes, until the oats have toasted.

3. Fill the bowls with the fresh fruit and sprinkle with the toasted oats. Serve with dollops of coconut yogurt.

PER SERVING : 496 CALS | 21.6G FAT | 16.9G SAT FAT | 70.6G CARBS | 34.3G SUGAR | 13.2G FIBER | 9.5G PROTEIN | 40MG SODIUM

MORNING POWERBOWL SMOOTHIE

HERE'S A GREAT WAY TO INCREASE YOUR NUTRIENT INTAKE, WITH PLENTY OF COLORFUL FRUITS TO PROVIDE ANTIOXIDANTS, AND HEALTHY FATS FROM NUTS AND SEEDS.

10 mins, plus chilling

None

1

1. Put the strawberries, blackberries, raspberries, half the banana, the hemp milk, coconut oil, and ground almonds into a blender and blend until smooth.

INGREDIENTS

⅓ cup hulled strawberries

⅓ cup blackberries

⅓ cup raspberries

1 banana, peeled

⅔ cup hemp milk

1 tablespoon coconut oil

1 tablespoon ground almonds
(almond meal)

1 kiwi, peeled and sliced

2 teaspoons chia seeds

1 small mango, peeled, pitted and chopped

1 tablespoon chopped walnuts

2 teaspoons toasted sesame seeds

2. Pour into a bowl and place the remaining ingredients on top to serve.

Replace the topping with fruits and nuts of your choice, aiming to use those in season—luscious berries would be great in the summer, sprinkled with freshly shredded mint leaves.

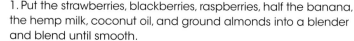

PER SERVING : 654 CALS | 34.4G FAT | 13.8G SAT FAT | 86.9G CARBS | 51.1G SUGAR | 19.5G FIBER | 11.1G PROTEIN | 40MG SODIUM

LAYERED POWERBOWL SMOOTHIE

THE COMBINATION OF FLAVORS IN THIS COLORFUL SMOOTHIE IS DELICIOUS! RICH IN ANTIOXIDANTS FROM THE FRUITS AND PROTEIN FROM THE ALMONDS AND SESAME SEEDS, IT MAKES A GREAT BREAKFAST.

15 mins | None | 2

INGREDIENTS

1 large mango, peeled and chopped

2 kiwis, peeled and chopped

½ teaspoon chlorella powder

1½ cups diced watermelon (with the seeds for additional vitamins)

1 tablespoon ground almonds (almond meal)

1 teaspoon sesame seeds

2 tablespoons gluten-free granola

¼ teaspoon ground cinnamon

1. Put the mango into a small blender and process until smooth. Divide between two glass bowls. Rinse the blender.

2. Put the kiwi and chlorella powder into the blender and process until smooth. Spoon the kiwi over the layer of mango in the bowls. Rinse the blender.

3. Put the watermelon into the blender and process until smooth. Add the ground almonds and sesame seeds and process briefly to combine. Spoon the watermelon over the kiwi mixture.

4. Sprinkle with the granola and ground cinnamon and serve.

PER SERVING : 303 CALS | 6.4G FAT | 1.1G SAT FAT | 61.3G CARBS | 44.2G SUGAR | 7.1G FIBER | 6.4G PROTEIN | TRACE SODIUM

GRAPES, KIWI & SPINACH SMOOTHIE BOWL

THIS HEALTH-IN-A-BOWL DISH IS BURSTING WITH NUTRIENT-PACKED NUTS, VITAMIN-FILLED FRUITS, AND LOADS OF GOODNESS. PERFECT AS A PICK-ME-UP OR AFTER A HEAVY MAIN DISH.

INGREDIENTS

1⅓ cups green grapes, frozen

2 kiwis, peeled and frozen

1 banana

1¾ cups fresh spinach leaves

1 cup water

juice of ½ lime

2 tablespoons sliced almonds, to decorate

2 tablespoons chia seeds, to decorate

¾ cup raspberries, to decorate

1. Transfer the frozen grapes, kiwi, banana, and spinach leaves to a food processor and blend until smooth. Add water until a thick smoothie consistency is reached. Taste and add lime juice to your preference.

2. Heat a small skillet over medium heat and add the sliced almonds. Toast for 1–2 minutes, until just brown. Set aside.

3. Pour the smoothie into bowls and decorate with the almonds, chia seeds, and raspberries.

PER SERVING : 349 CALS | 12G FAT | 1.1G SAT FAT | 59.5G CARBS | 31.7G SUGAR | 16.1G FIBER | 8.7G PROTEIN | TRACE SODIUM

BUCKWHEAT BREAKFAST BOWL

BUCKWHEAT HAS BEEN EATEN SINCE PALEOLITHIC TIMES. IT MAKES A TASTY CEREAL AND, BEING A SOURCE OF COMPLEX CARBOHYDRATES, PROVIDES AN EXCELLENT BOOST OF ENERGY.

20–25 mins, plus soaking and standing

INGREDIENTS

1 cup buckwheat

2 cups cold water

1¾ cups coconut yogurt

grated zest and juice of 1 orange

3 tablespoons goji berries

¾ cup raspberries

1 Granny Smith apple, cored and diced

1 tablespoon pumpkin seeds

2 passion fruits, pulp only

2 teaspoons ground cinnamon

½ teaspoon ground turmeric

seeds from 1 pomegranate

2 tablespoons agave syrup

1. Rinse the buckwheat three times in fresh water to clean the groats. Put into a bowl with the cold water. Soak for 20 minutes. Let stand for 30 minutes.

2. Drain and rinse the buckwheat, and let stand at room temperature—in either a sprouting tray or a strainer with a bowl beneath—for 36 hours. Rinse the buckwheat if the groats look sticky, and then once again before using.

3. Rinse, drain, and divide the buckwheat among four bowls. Divide the yogurt, sprinkle each bowl with the remaining ingredients, and serve.

This recipe uses buckwheat that has been sprouted for 36 hours; it can be done in less time, but a longer period provides optimum nutrition.

PER SERVING : 452 CALS | 22.4G FAT | 17.5G SAT FAT | 58G CARBS | 22.8G SUGAR | 9.8G FIBER | 10.1G PROTEIN |40MG SODIUM

BEET & POMEGRANATE SMOOTHIE BOWL

TENDER BEET AND ZESTY POMEGRANATE SEEDS ARE A FABULOUS COMBINATION. THE ADDITION OF SPINACH AND WHEATGRASS MAKES THIS TASTY BREAKFAST BOWL TRULY HEALTHY.

10 mins, plus optional chilling

None

INGREDIENTS

1 large beet, peeled and chopped

½ cup spinach leaves

3 tablespoons pomegranate seeds

½ cup water

juice of 1 orange

1 tablespoon raw honey

½ cup raw coconut yogurt (see below)

1 teaspoon wheatgrass powder

2 teaspoons buckwheat groats

2 round orange slices, halved

RAW COCONUT YOGURT

1 cup fresh or frozen coconut meat, thawed if frozen

½ cup raw coconut water

1 probiotic powder capsule

1. To make the yogurt, pour the coconut mixture into a bowl, cover with plastic wrap or foil, and let stand in the kitchen overnight at warm room temperature. In the morning, you should have about 1¼ cups of yogurt. Remove what you need and the rest will keep in the refrigerator for up to a week.

2. Put the beet into a blender with the spinach, 2 tablespoons of the pomegranate seeds, and half the water. Blend the contents until smooth.

3. Add the rest of the water, the orange juice, honey, three-quarters of the yogurt, and the wheatgrass powder to the blender. Blend again.

4. Pour the smoothie into a serving bowl and chill for an hour or so, if you have time.

5. Drizzle the remaining yogurt over the smoothie. Sprinkle the groats over the top and decorate with the orange slices and remaining seeds.

You can try raspberries instead of pomegranate seeds for a change, or if you want to make this smoothie when pomegranates aren't in season.

PER SERVING : 604 CALS | 32.7G FAT | 28G SAT FAT | 75.7G CARBS | 48.6G SUGAR | 17.6G FIBER | 10.2G PROTEIN | 160MG SODIUM

MATCHA POWER SMOOTHIE

THIS IS ONE OF THE BEST GREEN SMOOTHIES YOU'LL EVER TRY—IT'S BURSTING WITH SUPER INGREDIENTS, INCLUDING SPINACH AND AVOCADO, TO JUMP-START YOUR DAY.

5 mins, plus
optional
chilling

None

INGREDIENTS

1 cup spinach

1 banana, peeled and chopped

1 small ripe avocado, peeled, pitted, and coarsely chopped

2 kiwis, peeled and chopped

½ cup raw almond milk

½ tablespoon raw honey

½ teaspoon matcha green tea powder

½ teaspoon wheatgrass powder

2 teaspoons slivered almonds

½ teaspoon maca powder

1. Blend the spinach, banana, avocado, and one of the kiwis in a blender with half the milk until you have a puree.

2. Add the honey, matcha, wheatgrass, and remaining milk to the blender and blend until smooth. Pour the smoothie into your serving bowl. Chill for an hour if you have time.

3. Top your smoothie with the remaining kiwi and decorate with the slivered almonds and maca powder.

Matcha is a Japanese green tea rich in an antioxidant that fights cancers and heart disease. The powder gives you the full benefit of the leaves that you don't get by drinking the tea and discarding the leaves.

PER SERVING : 566 CALS | 30.3G FAT | 3.3G SAT FAT | 72.1G CARBS | 37.4G SUGAR | 18.9G FIBER | 13.2G PROTEIN | 40MG SODIUM

SWEET POTATO & KALE BREAKFAST BOWL

THIS FILLING BREAKFAST BOWL IS FULL OF GOODNESS—COLORFUL STEAMED VEGETABLES TOSSED WITH WARMING SPICES AND TOPPED WITH A POACHED EGG AND A SPRINKLING OF NUTS.

INGREDIENTS

2 large or 3 medium sweet potatoes, peeled and cut into chunks

3 cups chopped kale

2 eggs

2 teaspoons coconut oil

1 teaspoon cumin seeds

1 teaspoon mustard seeds

1 teaspoon pepper

½ teaspoon ground turmeric

¼ cup chopped walnuts

3 tablespoons blanched almonds, chopped

2¾ tablespoons pumpkin seeds

1. Put the sweet potatoes into a steamer and steam for 5–6 minutes, until tender. Add the kale to the steamer for the last 2 minutes of cooking.

2. Meanwhile, bring a small saucepan of water to a boil, break the eggs into a cup, one at a time, add to the pan and poach for 4–5 minutes.

3. Heat the oil in a large skillet or wok and add the cumin seeds, mustard seeds, pepper, and turmeric. Cook until the mustard seeds begin to "pop," then add the steamed vegetables and toss.

4. Divide the spiced vegetables between two warm bowls and top each one with a poached egg.

5. Sprinkle each serving with walnuts, almonds, and pumpkin seeds and serve immediately.

PER SERVING : 571 CALS | 31.8G FAT | 7.9G SAT FAT | 56.7G CARBS | 11.9G SUGAR | 13.1G FIBER | 22.7G PROTEIN | 200MG SODIUM

FRUITY SWEET POTATO BREAKFAST BOWL

NOT ONLY ARE SWEET POTATOES "SWEET" IN TASTE, THEY ALSO ADD GREAT NUTRIENTS AND A DELICIOUSLY CREAMY TEXTURE TO THIS UPLIFTINGLY COLORFUL BREAKFAST.

INGREDIENTS

2 medium sweet potatoes

1 tablespoon sunflower seeds

1 tablespoon pumpkin seeds

¼ cup plain yogurt

1 small banana, peeled and sliced

⅓ cup blueberries

½ cup red currants (or extra blueberries if difficult to find)

2 teaspoons goji berries

pinch of ground ginger

2 tablespoons maple syrup

1. Preheat the oven to 400°F. Prick the sweet potatoes all over with a fork or sharp knife and bake in the preheated oven for 40–45 minutes, until tender.

2. Meanwhile, dry-fry the sunflower seeds and pumpkin seeds in a skillet until they start to pop. Transfer to a plate to cool.

3. Place a sweet potato in each of two bowls and cut in half. Place a dollop of yogurt on each half, then add the banana, blueberries, red currants, and goji berries and sprinkle with toasted seeds.

4. Sprinkle with ginger and drizzle with maple syrup to serve.

You can top with fruits and toasted nuts or seeds of your choice; another great combination is pineapple, mango, and melon with toasted coconut flakes.

PER SERVING : 383 CALS | 6.2G FAT | 1.3G SAT FAT | 78G CARBS | 34.6G SUGAR | 10.2G FIBER | 7.8G PROTEIN | 120MG SODIUM

WAKE-UP SALAD

WHEN YOU WANT SOMETHING FOR BREAKFAST THAT ISN'T SWEET, TRY THIS CRUNCHY SALAD. IT'S LAYERED WITH DIFFERENT FRUITS AND VEGETABLES—PLUS IT'S QUICK TO PUT TOGETHER!

INGREDIENTS

2 cups chopped kale

1 red-skinned apple, cored and sliced

1 carrot, peeled and thinly sliced

4 Medjool dates, pitted and chopped

2 tablespoons chopped raw walnuts

2 teaspoons sesame seeds

2 teaspoons unhulled hemp seeds

2 teaspoons sunflower seeds

DRESSING

3 tablespoons cold-pressed
extra virgin canola oil

1 tablespoon raw apple cider vinegar

2 teaspoons stone-ground mustard

2 teaspoons maple syrup

½ teaspoon sea salt

½ teaspoon black pepper

2 scallions, finely chopped

1. To make the dressing, combine the dressing ingredients in a lidded jar or small mixing bowl. Shake or stir well.

2. Put the kale into a serving bowl or two individual dishes. Add the apple and carrot, and stir in the dates and walnuts.

3. Pour the dressing over the salad and mix together. Sprinkle with the seeds to serve.

Hemp seeds are a great source of antioxidants. This recipe has unhulled seeds for a richer mineral and fiber content, but you can also use hulled seeds—both are widely available.

PER SERVING : 555 CALS | 31.9G FAT | 2.5G SAT FAT | 66.2G CARBS | 49.6G SUGAR | 10.1G FIBER | 8.6G PROTEIN | 680MG SODIUM

OATMEAL WITH SALMON & AVOCADO

ROLLED OATS DON'T NEED TO BE SERVED SWEET TO BE TASTY. THEY PROVIDE SUSTAINED ENERGY THROUGHOUT THE MORNING, AND ADDING SALMON PROVIDES A PROTEIN AND OMEGA-3 BOOST.

INGREDIENTS

2 cups rolled oats

1½ cups milk

2½ cups water

4 eggs

4 teaspoons creamed horseradish

7 ounces hot smoked salmon, flaked

2 avocados, pitted, peeled, and sliced

freshly milled black pepper (optional)

2 tablespoons pumpkin seeds, toasted, to garnish

1. Put the oats into a saucepan with the milk and water. Bring to a boil, then simmer for 4–5 minutes, until thick and creamy.

2. Meanwhile, poach the eggs in a saucepan of simmering water for 4–5 minutes.

3. Stir the creamed horseradish and half the smoked salmon into the oatmeal.

4. Divide the oatmeal among four warm bowls and top each one with slices of avocado, a poached egg, and the remaining salmon.

5. Serve the oatmeal sprinkled with toasted pumpkin seeds and seasoned with pepper, if using.

Sautéed mushrooms with a fried egg and a sprinkling of chives make a delicious topping variation.

PER SERVING : 547 CALS | 32.8G FAT | 7.1G SAT FAT | 37.9G CARBS | 6G SUGAR | 9.1G FIBER | 27.7G PROTEIN | 520MG SODIUM

LIGHT LUNCHES

TOMATO, RICOTTA & GRILLED BREAD BOWL

THIS IS A DELICIOUS SUMMERY SALAD, USING ARTISAN TOMATOES, BASIL, AND CREAMY RICOTTA—A PERFECT COMBINATION. USE RIPE TOMATOES FOR AN INTENSE FLAVOR.

12 mins | 10–13 mins | 2

INGREDIENTS

2 tablespoons olive oil

1 zucchini, thickly sliced

4 slices ciabatta

2 teaspoons balsamic vinegar

6 basil leaves, shredded

2 extra-small yellow tomatoes, halved or cut into wedges

6 cherry tomatoes, halved or quartered

1 garlic clove, peeled but left whole

¼ teaspoon cumin seeds

⅓ cup ricotta cheese

1 tablespoon pistachio nuts, chopped

1. Heat a ridged grill pan until hot.

2. Brush 1 tablespoon of the oil over both sides of the zucchini slices and the bread.

3. Place the zucchini and bread in the pan and cook for 4–5 minutes on each side, until they have chargrilled marks. Remove from the pan and set aside until needed.

4. Meanwhile, in a large bowl, whisk together the remaining oil, the vinegar, and basil. Add the tomatoes and toss, then let stand until the zucchini are cooked.

5. Add the zucchini to the bowl and toss. Rub each slice of bread with the garlic.

6. Toast the cumin seeds in a dry skillet for 2–3 minutes, until they release their aroma. Stir into the ricotta cheese.

7. Divide the tomato mixture between two bowls. Top with the spiced ricotta cheese and a sprinkling of the chopped nuts and serve with the toasts on the side.

PER SERVING : 640 CALS | 33.2G FAT | 11.1G SAT FAT | 60.4G CARBS | 9.6G SUGAR | 5.9G FIBER | 25.5G PROTEIN | 440MG SODIUM

SPRING ROLL BOWL WITH SWEET GARLIC LIME SAUCE

THIS LIGHT, SUMMER DISH, DELIGHTFULLY RICH IN COLOR, IS QUICK TO PREPARE—
THE ONLY SIGNIFICANT PREPARATION IS CUTTING UP THE VEGETABLES.

12 mins · 4 mins · 2

INGREDIENTS

10½ ounces ready-to-wok rice noodles

1 avocado, pitted, peeled, and sliced

6 cherry tomatoes, halved

¼ cucumber, halved, seeded, and sliced

4 radishes, thinly sliced

⅓ cup chopped peanuts

2–3 fresh mint sprigs

2–3 fresh cilantro sprigs

DRESSING

2 tablespoons extra virgin olive oil

½ teaspoon sesame oil

juice and zest of ½ lime

½ teaspoon maple syrup

1 garlic clove, crushed

1. Put the noodles into a bowl and add boiling water. Let stand for 4 minutes, or according to the package directions, then drain.

2. To make the dressing, whisk together the olive oil, sesame oil, lime juice and zest, maple syrup, and garlic.

3. Divide the noodles between two bowls and top with the avocado, tomatoes, cucumber, radishes, peanuts, mint, and cilantro.

4. Pour the dressing over the top to serve.

Always use good-quality extra virgin olive oil when making a dressing for the flavor and nutrients it will provide. Olive oil is rich in omega 3 oils, important for brain and cell health.

PER SERVING : 650 CALS | 41.8G FAT | 5.6G SAT FAT | 64.9G CARBS | 7.7G SUGAR | 11.1G FIBER | 10.1G PROTEIN | 40MG SODIUM

VEGETABLE RICE BOWL

THIS RECIPE INCLUDES A HOMEMADE CHILI SAUCE—YOU CAN MAKE IT AS HOT AS YOU DARE! THE RECIPE ALSO WORKS WELL WITH SHRIMP, CHICKEN, OR SHREDDED BEEF.

20 mins, plus cooling and marinating

20 mins

INGREDIENTS

1 tablespoon soy sauce

1 tablespoon sesame oil

1 teaspoon honey

10½ ounces tofu, cut into cubes

2 tablespoons sunflower oil

1½ cups basmati or other long-grain rice

1 large carrot, peeled and sliced into thin strips

7 ounces cremini mushrooms, sliced

½ cup shredded snow peas

2 cups baby spinach leaves

4 eggs

1 tablespoon black sesame seeds, to garnish

CHILI SAUCE

2–3 red chiles, seeded and finely chopped

3 garlic cloves, crushed

¼ cup white wine vinegar

2 tablespoons sugar

2 tablespoons sunflower oil

1. To make the chili sauce, put the chiles, garlic cloves, vinegar, and sugar into a small saucepan and bring to a boil. Remove from the heat and let cool, then stir in 2 tablespoons of sunflower oil. Set aside.

2. Combine the soy sauce, sesame oil, and honey and put into a nonmetallic bowl with the tofu—let marinate for 10 minutes.

3. Cook the rice according to the package directions. Drain. Meanwhile, heat 1 tablespoon of the sunflower oil in a saucepan, add the carrots and mushrooms, and cook for 4–5 minutes, until soft. Transfer to a plate with a slotted spoon.

4. Put the cooked rice into the pan, then add the marinated tofu, carrots, mushrooms, snow peas, and spinach. Cover and cook for 2–3 minutes.

5. Meanwhile, heat the remaining sunflower oil in a skillet, add the eggs, and cook to your liking. Divide the mixture among four bowls. Top each one with a fried egg and spoonful of chili sauce, sprinkle with the sesame seeds, and serve.

PER SERVING : 698 CALS | 20.2G FAT | 5G SAT FAT | 81.3G CARBS | 12.6G SUGAR | 4.8G FIBER | 27.4G PROTEIN | 0.8G SODIUM

TOFU & SWEET POTATO BOWL

BECAUSE OF THEIR INTENSE COLOR, THE SWEET POTATOES IN THIS REFRESHING BOWL ARE RICH IN ANTIOXIDANTS. TRY TO EAT THEM INSTEAD OF WHITE POTATOES, WHICH ARE RICH IN STARCH.

15 mins, plus marinating

35–40 mins

4

INGREDIENTS

1 tablespoon soy sauce

1 tablespoon honey

1 tablespoon cumin seeds

13 ounces tofu, cut into strips or chunks

1 sweet potato, chopped

1 red onion, cut into wedges

2 carrots, chopped

1 tablespoon olive oil

3½ cups baby spinach leaves

½ cup shredded sugar snap peas

2 tablespoons pumpkin seeds, toasted

DRESSING

½ cup hazelnuts, toasted

¼ cup extra virgin olive oil

juice of ½ orange

juice of ½ lemon

2 teaspoons sherry vinegar

1. Preheat the oven to 400°F.

2. Mix the soy sauce, honey, and cumin seeds together, add the tofu to the mixture, and let marinate for 30 minutes.

3. Meanwhile, put the sweet potato, onion, and carrots into a roasting pan, drizzle with olive oil, and roast in the preheated oven for 35–40 minutes, until tender and slightly charred at the edges.

4. To make the dressing, put the hazelnuts into a food processor and process until finely chopped. Put into a bowl with the extra virgin olive oil, orange juice, lemon juice, and vinegar and mix to combine.

5. Preheat a wok until hot, then drain the tofu, discarding the marinade. Add the tofu to the wok and stir-fry for 4–5 minutes.

6. Divide the spinach among four bowls and top with the roasted vegetables and tofu. Sprinkle with the shredded peas and the pumpkin seeds and drizzle with the dressing to serve.

PER SERVING : 537 CALS | 40.8G FAT | 4.8G SAT FAT | 28.4G CARBS | 11.7G SUGAR | 7.8G FIBER | 22.2G PROTEIN | 280MG SODIUM

CRUNCHY NOODLE BEANFEAST

THIS BRIGHT, SUMMERY SALAD HAS DIFFERENT LAYERS OF TEXTURES AND CRUNCH TO DISCOVER AS YOU WORK THROUGH YOUR BEANFEAST BOWL!

20 mins · 5 mins · 4

INGREDIENTS

7 ounces vermicelli rice noodles

1½ cups canned lima beans, drained and rinsed

1 large carrot, peeled and cut into julienne strips

1 red chile, seeded and finely sliced

½ cup shredded snow peas

¼ cucumber, cut into julienne strips

4 baby corn, halved lengthwise

2 tablespoons cashew nuts

¾ cup bean sprouts

⅓ cup fresh mint leaves

⅓ cup fresh cilantro leaves

⅓ cup fresh Thai basil leaves

2 tablespoons sesame seeds, toasted

DRESSING

2 tablespoons packed brown sugar

2 tablespoons Thai fish sauce

juice of 2 limes

1 garlic clove, crushed

1. Cook the noodles according to the package directions. Drain and put into a bowl.

2. To make the dressing, put the sugar, fish sauce, and lime juice into a small bowl and stir until the sugar has dissolved. Stir in the garlic.

3. Add all the remaining ingredients apart from the toasted sesame seeds to the noodles, pour in the dressing, and toss together well.

4. Serve in four bowls, sprinkled with the toasted sesame seeds.

PER SERVING : 378 CALS | 5G FAT | 0.6G SAT FAT | 69.9G CARBS | 13.1G SUGAR | 6.5G FIBER | 12.6G PROTEIN | 880MG SODIUM

COUSCOUS WITH ROASTED TOMATOES & PINE NUTS

THE MEDITERRANEAN FLAVORS OF ROASTED TOMATOES, FRESH MINT, TOASTED PINE NUTS, AND FETA CHEESE COME TOGETHER IN THIS SIMPLE SUMMER DISH.

10 mins,
plus 10 mins
standing

8 mins

4

INGREDIENTS

2 cups cherry tomatoes

3 tablespoons olive oil

¾ cup couscous

1 cup boiling water

¼ cup pine nuts, toasted

⅓ cup coarsely chopped fresh mint

finely grated zest of 1 lemon

½ tablespoons lemon juice

salt and pepper (optional)

crisp green salad, to serve (optional)

vegetarian feta cheese, to serve (optional)

1. Preheat the oven to 425°F. Put the tomatoes and 1 tablespoon of the oil into a ovenproof dish. Toss together, then roast in the preheated oven for 7–8 minutes, until the tomatoes are soft and the skins have burst. Let stand for 5 minutes.

2. Put the couscous into a heatproof bowl. Pour boiling water over the grains, cover, and let stand for 8–10 minutes, or according to the package directions, until soft and the liquid has been absorbed.

3. Fluff up the couscous with a fork.

4. Add the tomatoes and their juices, the pine nuts, mint, lemon zest, lemon juice, and the remaining oil. Season with salt and pepper, if using, then gently toss together.

5. Serve the couscous warm or cold, with a green salad and some feta cheese, if liked.

PER SERVING : 374 CALS | 23.2G FAT | 7.1G SAT FAT | 31.8G CARBS | 4.4G SUGAR | 4.1G FIBER | 11.3G PROTEIN | 320MG SODIUM

CHARGRILLED VEGETABLE BOWL

ROASTING VEGETABLES BRINGS OUT THEIR FLAVOR—COOK THEM
TO JUST CHAR THE EDGES, SLIGHTLY CARAMELIZING THEM.

INGREDIENTS

1 yellow zucchini, trimmed and sliced

1 green zucchini, trimmed and sliced

3½ ounces asparagus, trimmed and halved

1 red bell pepper, seeded and chopped

1 yellow bell pepper, seeded and chopped

1 red onion, cut into 8 wedges

1 fennel bulb, trimmed and sliced

¼ cup olive oil

2 teaspoons cumin seeds

16 sprigs watercress

4 fresh mint sprigs

HUMMUS

¾ cup drained and rinsed, canned chickpeas

½ cup walnuts

2 tablespoons lemon juice

2 garlic cloves, crushed

2 tablespoons tahini

3–4 tablespoons water

½ teaspoon paprika

salt and pepper (optional)

1. Preheat the oven to 400°F.

2. Divide the chopped and sliced vegetables between two roasting pans and drizzle each one with 1 tablespoon of the oil and 1 teaspoon of the cumin seeds. Toss well to coat the vegetables with the oil. Season with salt and pepper, if using.

3. Roast the vegetables in the preheated oven for 35–40 minutes, until they start to char at the edges.

4. Meanwhile, to make the hummus, put the chickpeas and walnuts into a food processor and process until broken down.

5. With the machine running, add the lemon juice and then the garlic, tahini, and remaining oil. Add 3–4 tablespoons of water to loosen and then add the paprika and salt and pepper, if using.

6. Divide the watercress and roasted vegetables among four bowls, then top with a dollop of walnut hummus. Sprinkle with mint sprigs to serve.

PER SERVING : 348 CALS | 28.7G FAT | 3.3G SAT FAT | 21.8G CARBS | 10.2G SUGAR | 7.6G FIBER | 7.9G PROTEIN | 40MG SODIUM

VIETNAMESE SUMMER ROLL BOWL

THESE DECONSTRUCTED VIETNAMESE SUMMER ROLLS MADE WITH VEGETABLES, AROMATIC LEAVES, SUCCULENT SHRIMP, AND LIGHT RICE NOODLES ARE A PERFECT SUMMER LUNCH DISH.

INGREDIENTS

7 ounces rice vermicelli noodles

20 fresh mint leaves

20 fresh cilantro leaves

8 fresh Thai basil sprigs, leaves only

8 snipped fresh chives

16 cooked large jumbo shrimp

1 carrot, grated

½ cucumber, cut into matchsticks

2 Boston lettuce, leaves separated

¼ cup salted peanuts, chopped

SAUCE

1½ tablespoons sugar

¼ cup lime juice

2 tablespoons Thai fish sauce

2 garlic cloves, crushed

1 fresh Thai chile, finely sliced

1. Put the noodles into a large bowl and pour boiling water over them. Let soak for 4–5 minutes, or according to package directions, then rinse in cold water and drain.

2. Meanwhile, to make the sauce, whisk together the sugar, lime juice, Thai fish sauce, garlic, and chil until the sugar is dissolved.

3. Toss the noodles with the herbs, then divide among four bowls.

4. Top with the remaining ingredients, then pour the sauce over the bowls to serve.

Instead of shrimp, you can use shredded pork or chicken. Always use fresh herbs—mint, cilantro, dill, and parsley all work well.

PER SERVING : 426 CALS | 7.3G FAT | 1.4G SAT FAT | 59.2G CARBS | 9.8G SUGAR | 4.5G FIBER | 30. 8G PROTEIN | 1,880MG SODIUM

CUCUMBER & BUCKWHEAT YOGURT

RAW COCONUT YOGURT IS A WONDERFUL BASE FOR ALL KINDS OF DISHES. MAKE THIS CRUNCHY AND REFRESHING YOGURT JAR FOR AN EASY LUNCH OR LIGHT BITE ON THE GO.

10 mins, plus soaking and chilling

None

INGREDIENTS

1 cucumber, halved, seeded, and chopped

2 cups raw coconut yogurt (see below)

3 tablespoons chopped fresh mint

1 teaspoon sea salt

1 teaspoon black pepper

⅔ cup sun-dried raisins

⅔ cup chopped raw walnuts

¾ cup raw buckwheat groats, soaked in water for 20 minutes, drained, and rinsed

20 fresh mint leaves, to garnish

RAW COCONUT YOGURT

1 cup fresh or frozen coconut meat, thawed if frozen

½ cup raw coconut water

1 probiotic powder capsule

1. Pour the coconut mixture into a bowl, cover with plastic wrap or foil, and let stand in the kitchen overnight at warm room temperature. In the morning, you should have about 1¼ cups of yogurt. Remove what you need and the rest will keep in the refrigerator for up to a week.

2. Wrap the cucumber pieces in paper towels and squeeze to release the moisture—the paper towels should end up soaked.

3. Mix the yogurt, mint, salt, and pepper together in a bowl.

4. Divide the ingredients evenly among four lidded jars with a 9 oz–9 ¾ fluid-ounce capacity. Layer with the raisins, half the walnuts, the soaked groats, three-quarters of the cucumber, and the yogurt mixture. Add the remaining cucumber and walnuts as a garnish.

5. Divide the mint leaves among each of the jars and chill for 30 minutes before serving.

Try finely chopped scallions instead of the mint and add ½ teaspoon of crushed garlic to the yogurt mixture. Fresh, green, new-season's garlic is best.

PER SERVING : 659 CALS | 45G FAT | 29.3G SAT FAT | 63.4G CARBS | 23.6G SUGAR | 15.2G FIBER | 12G PROTEIN | 640MG SODIUM

SEAWEED POWER BOWL

SEAWEED IS AN EXTRAORDINARY SOURCE OF IODINE, A NUTRIENT MISSING IN ALMOST EVERY OTHER FOOD. IODINE IS CRITICALLY IMPORTANT TO MAINTAINING A HEALTHY THYROID.

20 mins, plus standing

None

INGREDIENTS

¾ ounce dried kelp

½ cucumber

2 oranges

1 red chile, seeded and finely diced

2 carrots, grated

1 large mango, peeled, pitted, and chopped

3 heads of bok choy, chopped

⅓ cup fresh mint leaves

⅓ cup fresh cilantro leaves

2 tablespoons salted peanuts, chopped

DRESSING

3 tablespoons olive oil

grated zest and juice of 1 lime

1 teaspoon honey

1 teaspoon miso paste

1. Put the kelp into a bowl of water and let stand for 10 minutes to rehydrate.

2. Meanwhile, to make the dressing, whisk together the oil, lime zest and juice, honey, and miso paste.

3. Halve the cucumber lengthwise and, using a teaspoon, scoop out and discard the seeds.

4. Peel the oranges and cut them into sections.

5. Coarsely chop the kelp and put into a large bowl with the cucumber, orange sections, chile, carrot, mango, bok choy, and half the mint and cilantro.

6. Pour in the dressing and toss well. Divide among four bowls.

7. Sprinkle each bowl with chopped peanuts and the remaining mint and cilantro.

PER SERVING : 252 CALS | 13.4G FAT | 1.9G SAT FAT | 31G CARBS | 22.2G SUGAR | 6.4G FIBER | 4.8G PROTEIN | 160MG SODIUM

SUSHI ROLL BOWL

SUSHI IS A GREAT HEALTHY SNACK OR MEAL: THE FISH HAS OMEGA-3 FATS; RICE PROVIDES ENERGY AND PROTEIN; SEAWEED, RICH IN IODINE, IS VITAL FOR A HEALTHY THYROID. AND IT TASTES GREAT!

15 mins,
plus
cooling

10 mins

INGREDIENTS

1⅔ cups glutinous rice

2 tablespoons rice vinegar

1 teaspoon sugar

1 large avocado, peeled, pitted, and sliced

7 ounces raw tuna, sliced

7 ounces raw salmon, sliced

juice of ½ lemon

4 sheets nori seaweed, shredded

¼ cucumber, cut into matchsticks

2 tablespoons snipped fresh chives

1 tablespoon black sesame seeds

¼ cup gluten-free soy sauce

1. Cook the rice according to the package directions. When all the water has been absorbed and the rice is cooked, stir through the vinegar and sugar, then cover and let cool.

2. Divide the rice among four bowls.

3. Top each bowl with slices of avocado, tuna and salmon.

4. Squeeze the lemon juice over the top, then add the nori, cucumber, chives, and sesame seeds.

5. Serve with the soy sauce.

PER SERVING : 572 CALS | 17.7G FAT | 3.1G SAT FAT | 70.1G CARBS | 2.2G SUGAR | 7.6G FIBER | 32G PROTEIN | 960MG SODIUM

PESTO SALMON WITH SPRING VEG BOWL

WITH A LITTLE GENTLE STEAMING AND A TASTY DRESSING, YOU CAN ENJOY YOUNG VEGETABLES. THIS LEMON DRESSING CUTS THROUGH THE RICHNESS OF THE PESTO SALMON PERFECTLY.

INGREDIENTS

1⅓ cups fresh or frozen peas

1⅓ cups fresh fava beans

7 ounces asparagus, woody stems discarded

7 ounces baby carrots, scrubbed

4 skinless salmon fillets, each weighing 5½ ounces

¼ cup pesto

2 tablespoons sunflower seeds, toasted

2 tablespoons pumpkin seeds, toasted

2 tablespoons shredded fresh basil

LEMON DRESSING

¼ cup extra virgin olive oil

grated zest and juice of 1 lemon

1. Put all the vegetables into a steamer and steam them for 10–12 minutes, until tender.

2. Meanwhile, preheat the broiler to hot and line a baking sheet with foil. Place the salmon on the prepared baking sheet and spoon the pesto over the fish. Cook under the broiler for 3–4 minutes on each side.

3. Mix the oil with the lemon zest and juice to make the lemon dressing, and toss with the cooked vegetables.

4. Divide the vegetables among four warm, shallow bowls and top each one with a salmon fillet.

5. Sprinkle with the sunflower seeds, pumpkin seeds, and shredded basil and serve.

PER SERVING : 646 CALS | 42.9G FAT | 7.6G SAT FAT | 21.9G CARBS | 7.7G SUGAR | 9.7G FIBER | 42G PROTEIN | 280MG SODIUM

TUNA POKE BOWL

A POKE BOWL IS A STAPLE HAWAIIAN DISH THAT NORMALLY CONTAINS RAW FISH AND ALL KINDS OF VIBRANT INGREDIENTS. THIS ONE INCLUDES TUNA AND WAKAME.

15 mins, plus soaking

25 mins

INGREDIENTS

7 oz brown rice

½ ounce wakame, soaked in lukewarm water for 10–15 minutes and coarsely chopped

2 tablespoons gluten-free soy sauce

2 tablespoons rice wine vinegar

8 ounces good-quality raw tuna, sliced

1 avocado, pitted, peeled, and sliced

8 cherry tomatoes, halved

4 scallions, thinly sliced

½ teaspoon crushed red pepper flakes

2 tablespoons olive oil

1 tablespoon black sesame seeds

1. Cook the rice according to the package directions.

2. Put the cooked rice into a bowl and stir in half the soaked wakame, half the soy sauce, and the rice wine vinegar. Divide among four bowls and top with the tuna, avocado, tomatoes, and scallions.

3. Mix the remaining soy sauce and wakame with the crushed red pepper flakes, olive oil, and sesame seeds in a small bowl. Sprinkle the dressing over the poke bowls to serve.

If you don't want to eat your fish raw, flash-fry it quickly in a skillet before adding to your dish.

PER SERVING : 399 CALS | 15.4G FAT | 2.2G SAT FAT | 45.5G CARBS | 2.4G SUGAR | 5.3G FIBER | 20.4G PROTEIN | 520MG SODIUM

SPICY CHICKEN NOODLE SOUP

THIS QUICK, WHOLESOME SOUP IS A WINNER FOR AN INSTANT MEAL THAT'S PACKED WITH GOODNESS. THE MAIN FLAVOR COMES FROM MISO, A HIGHLY NUTRITIOUS FERMENTED PASTE.

INGREDIENTS

1¼ cups chicken broth

1 tablespoon miso paste

¾-inch piece fresh ginger, peeled and finely grated

1 red chile, seeded and thinly sliced

1 carrot, cut into thin strips

3 cups coarsely chopped bok choy

5½ ounces dried egg cellophane noodles, cooked

1 cooked chicken breast, shredded

dash of dark soy sauce

4 scallions, trimmed and finely chopped

1. Put the broth and 1 cup of boiling water into a saucepan and bring to a boil over medium–high heat. Add the miso paste and simmer for 1–2 minutes.

2. Add the ginger, chile, carrot, bok choy, cooked noodles, and chicken. Simmer for an additional 4–5 minutes. Season with the soy sauce.

3. Sprinkle the scallions in the bottom of two serving dishes and pour the soup over them. Serve immediately.

PER SERVING : 511 CALS | 7.9G FAT | 2.3G SAT FAT | 66.4G CARBS | 7G SUGAR | 7.1G FIBER | 41.3G PROTEIN | 1,000MG SODIUM

KOREAN BULGOGI BOWL

THIS KOREAN BULGOGI RECIPE HAS LEAN HIGH-PROTEIN STEAK, BROWN RICE THAT LEAVES YOU FEELING FULLER FOR LONGER, AND VITAMIN-PACKED FRUIT AND VEG. IT'S ALSO A TASTE SENSATION.

15 mins plus marinating

30 mins

4

INGREDIENTS

1 pound 2 ounces flank or skirt steak, fat trimmed off and thinly sliced

1¼ cups long-grain brown rice

4 teaspoons sesame seeds

7 ounces baby broccoli, stems cut into thick slices and florets halved lengthwise

1–2 tablespoons sunflower oil

MARINADE

2 tablespoons reduced-sodium soy sauce

2 tablespoons rice wine vinegar

4 teaspoons molasses sugar

2 teaspoons gochujang Korean chili paste or other red chili paste

2 garlic cloves, finely chopped

2-inch piece fresh ginger, peeled and coarsely grated

1 apple, unpeeled, coarsely grated

TO SERVE

1½ cups coarsely grated carrot

1¼ cups thinly shredded red cabbage

½ small mango, diced

6 tablespoons kimchi

1 tablespoon fresh cilantro sprigs, torn

1. To make the marinade, add the soy sauce, vinegar, and sugar to a medium, shallow ceramic or glass bowl. Mix in the gochujang chili paste, garlic, ginger, and apple to form a smooth paste. Add the steak slices and toss together. Cover the bowl with plastic wrap and marinate in the refrigerator for at least 30 minutes–1 hour.

2. When almost ready to serve, add the rice to a saucepan of boiling water, bring the water back to a boil, then simmer for about 30 minutes, or according to package directions, until tender. Toast the sesame seeds in a dry skillet for 2–3 minutes, until just beginning to color, then remove the pan from the heat.

3. Add the baby broccoli florets and stems to a wok or large skillet with 2 tablespoons cold water, cover and cook for 2 minutes, then drain off the water, add 1 tablespoon of the oil, and stir-fry the broccoli over high heat for 1 minute. Remove from the pan and reserve.

4. Heat the remaining oil in the pan, drain the steak, reserving the marinade, then gradually add the steak slices to the hot wok until they are all in the pan and stir-fry over high heat for 2–3 minutes, until browned.

5. Pour in the remaining marinade and 2 tablespoons of cold water, then cook for 1–2 minutes to make a sauce.

6. Drain and spoon the hot just-cooked rice into four large serving bowls, top with the steak and baby broccoli, and sprinkle with the toasted sesame seeds. Add little piles of the grated carrot, shredded cabbage, diced mango, and kimchi to the bowls, then sprinkle with cilantro. Serve immediately.

PER SERVING : 667 CALS | 24.5G FAT | 6.9G SAT FAT | 70G CARBS | 18G SUGAR | 7.3G FIBER | 41.7G PROTEIN | 560MG SODIUM

CHICKEN & CHICKPEA POWER BOWL

CHICKEN AND CHICKPEAS ARE BOTH RICH IN PROTEIN, SO THIS RECIPE GIVES YOU A DOUBLE BOOST! WITH A LOVELY PEANUT DRESSING, THIS ONE IS HARD TO RESIST.

INGREDIENTS

1½ cups drained and rinsed, canned chickpeas

½ butternut squash, peeled, seeded, and chopped into bite-size pieces

2 red bell peppers, seeded and chopped

1 red onion, coarsely chopped

3 tablespoons olive oil

½ teaspoon paprika

½ teaspoon cumin seeds

2 large chicken breasts

20 sprigs fresh watercress, to serve

SAUCE

½ teaspoon peanut oil

1 garlic clove, crushed

½ teaspoon crushed red pepper flakes

½ tablespoon packed light brown sugar

1 teaspoon gluten-free soy sauce

2 tablespoons smooth peanut butter

1¼ cups coconut milk

1. Preheat the oven to 400°F.

2. Put the chickpeas, squash, red bell peppers, and onion into two roasting pans, add 1 tablespoon of olive oil to each pan, and toss to coat the vegetables. Roast in the preheated oven for 30–35 minutes, until the vegetables are tender and the edges charred.

3. Meanwhile, mix the remaining olive oil with the paprika and cumin seeds.

4. Place the chicken between two sheets of wax paper and flatten slightly with a rolling pin or mallet (this helps them cook more evenly).

5. Rub the chicken with the spiced oil. Preheat a ridged grill pan to hot.

6. Add the chicken to the pan and cook for 4–5 minutes on each side, until cooked through. Let rest for 1–2 minutes, then cut into strips.

7. Meanwhile, to make the sauce, heat the peanut oil in a saucepan, add the garlic and crushed red pepper flakes, and cook for 30 seconds, then add the sugar and cook for 1 minute. Stir in the soy sauce and peanut butter, then add the coconut milk, a little at a time, stirring constantly, until the sauce has the consistency you want.

8. Serve the roasted vegetables and chickpeas on a bed of watercress in four bowls, topped with strips of chicken and the sauce.

PER SERVING : 450 CALS | 20.8G FAT | 3.9G SAT FAT | 35G CARBS | 13G SUGAR | 8.1G FIBER | 30.6G PROTEIN | 80MG SODIUM

SALADS

COLORFUL COLESLAW

THIS COLESLAW IS FULL OF NUTRIENTS—FIBER, ANTIOXIDANTS, AND ESSENTIAL FATS. FOR A BALANCED MEAL, SERVE WITH GRILLED FISH OR BARBECUED CHICKEN.

25 mins | None | 4

1. To make the dressing, put the yogurt, mustard, lime juice, honey, and tahini into a large bowl and mix to combine.

2. Add the remaining ingredients and toss well to coat with the dressing.

INGREDIENTS

1 cup shredded red cabbage
1 cup shredded green cabbage
2 carrots, grated
1 small red onion, thinly sliced
1 red bell pepper, seeded and thinly sliced
1 yellow bell pepper, seeded and thinly sliced
1 fennel bulb, trimmed and shredded
4 radishes, thinly sliced
1 tablespoon chopped fresh basil
1 tablespoon chopped fresh parsley
1 tablespoon chopped fresh mint
3 tablespoons pine nuts, toasted
2 tablespoons hemp seeds, toasted

DRESSING

¼ cup plain yogurt
½ teaspoon Dijon mustard
juice of 1 lime
½ teaspoon honey
2 teaspoons tahini

For a balanced meal, serve this coleslaw with broiled fish, such as tuna or mackerel fillets. Or if you are having a summer barbecue, try it with barbecued chicken or pork chops.

PER SERVING : 174 CALS | 9.2G FAT | 1.1G SAT FAT | 19.4G CARBS | 10.2G SUGAR | 6G FIBER | 6.1G PROTEIN | 80MG SODIUM

CORN, RICE & BEAN BOWL

THIS ATTRACTIVE SALAD CAN BE SERVED WARM OR COLD. MIXING RICE AND BEANS PROVIDES A COMPLETE BALANCE OF PROTEIN FOR THE MEAL—PERFECT FOR VEGETARIANS.

INGREDIENTS

½ cup long-grain brown rice

½ cup wild rice

1½ cups canned mixed beans, such as kidney beans, pinto beans, and chickpeas, drained and rinsed,

1¼ cups frozen corn kernels, thawed

⅔ cup frozen peas, thawed

1 small red onion, finely sliced

⅓ cup pistachio nuts, chopped

1 large carrot, peeled and grated

1 large avocado, sliced

⅓ cup fresh cilantro leaves, to serve

salt and pepper (optional)

DRESSING

juice and zest of 1 lime

2 tablespoons extra virgin olive oil

1 teaspoon honey

1 red chile, seeded and diced

⅓ cup fresh mint leaves, chopped

1. Cook the rice according to the package directions.

2. Meanwhile, to make the dressing, whisk together the lime zest and juice, oil, honey, chile, and mint.

3. Drain the rice, place it in a large bowl and mix in the beans, corn, peas, onion, nuts and carrot. Stir in the dressing and season with salt and pepper, if using.

4. Divide among four bowls, top with the avocado slices, and sprinkle with cilantro leaves to serve.

So many things can be added to this bowl—choose your favorite beans, nuts, and vegetables. You could also add fruit—try chopped apricots or blueberries for added color.

PER SERVING : 579 CALS | 24.4G FAT | 3.4G SAT FAT | 77.9G CARBS | 9.6G SUGAR | 14.9G FIBER | 16.6G PROTEIN | 40MG SODIUM

LENTIL, GRAPE & FETA SALAD

THIS IS A FABULOUS COMBINATION—CREAMY FETA CHEESE WITH CRUNCHY
NUTS AND SWEET GRAPES, TOPPED WITH A CITRUS AND HERB DRESSING.

INGREDIENTS

1 romaine lettuce

1¼ cups arugula

⅓ cup seedless red grapes

⅓ cup seedless white grapes

1½ cups cooked green lentils

4 scallions, trimmed and sliced

1 red bell pepper, seeded and thinly sliced

¾ cup pecans

¾ cup crumbled feta cheese

DRESSING

3 tablespoons extra virgin olive oil

1 teaspoon walnut oil

1 teaspoon raspberry vinegar

juice of ½ lemon

2 teaspoons maple syrup

1 teaspoon whole-grain mustard

½ garlic clove, crushed

2 teaspoons chopped fresh mint

2 teaspoons chopped fresh parsley

salt and pepper (optional)

1. To make the dressing, whisk together the olive oil, walnut oil, vinegar, lemon juice, maple syrup, mustard, garlic, mint, and parsley. Season with salt and pepper, if using.

2. Divide the lettuce and arugula among four large, shallow bowls.

3. Halve the red grapes and white grapes. Mix the lentils, scallions, red grapes, white grapes, and red bell pepper together and spoon the mixture over the lettuce and arugula.

4. Chop the pecans, then sprinkle the nuts with the cheese over the salad, drizzle with the dressing, and serve immediately.

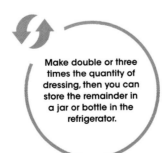

Make double or three times the quantity of dressing, then you can store the remainder in a jar or bottle in the refrigerator.

PER SERVING : 475 CALS | 32.8G FAT | 7.5G SAT FAT | 35.1G CARBS | 13.4G SUGAR | 12.5G FIBER | 16G PROTEIN | 320MG SODIUM

SUMMER ABUNDANCE SALAD

THIS RECIPE INCLUDES VEGETABLES, FRUIT, AND LEGUMES TO PROVIDE A BALANCED MEAL IN A BOWL, TOPPED WITH A DELICIOUS LEMON DRESSING TO BRING IT ALL TO LIFE.

INGREDIENTS

1 tablespoon sesame seeds

2 tablespoons pecans, coarsely chopped

1¾ cups arugula

1 large carrot, peeled

2 cooked beets, sliced

1 dessert apple, such as Gala, Pink Lady, or Golden Delicious, cored and sliced

1½ cups drained and rinsed, canned chickpeas

2 celery stalks, sliced

⅓ cup blackberries

⅓ cup alfalfa sprouts

DRESSING

3 tablespoons extra virgin olive oil

1 tablespoon lemon juice

grated zest of ½ lemon

½ teaspoon Dijon mustard

½ teaspoon honey

salt and pepper (optional)

1. Toast the seeds and nuts in a dry skillet until lightly golden.

2. To make the dressing, whisk together the oil, lemon juice, lemon zest, mustard, and honey in a bowl. Season with salt and pepper, if using.

3. Divide the arugula, carrot, beets, apple, chickpeas, celery, blackberries, and alfalfa sprouts among four bowls, then drizzle with the dressing and serve.

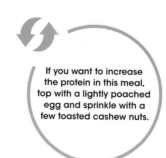

If you want to increase the protein in this meal, top with a lightly poached egg and sprinkle with a few toasted cashew nuts.

PER SERVING : 270 CALS | 16.3G FAT | 1.9G SAT FAT | 24.8G CARBS | 12.1G SUGAR | 7.6G FIBER | 6.6G PROTEIN | 80MG SODIUM

JEWEL SALAD WITH RANCH DRESSING

A BEAUTIFUL SALAD IS ALWAYS WELCOMED AT THE DINNER TABLE. THIS VIBRANT DISH IS COMPLEMENTED BY A PROTEIN-RICH VARIATION OF THE COUNTRY'S FAVORITE RANCH DRESSING.

20 mins, plus soaking · None · 4

INGREDIENTS

2 large tomatoes, seeded

1 cucumber

½ red onion

1 carrot

1 yellow bell pepper, seeded

10 red radishes

½ cup mixed chopped soft herbs, such as parsley, mint, and cilantro

zest and juice of ½ lemon

¼ cup cold-pressed extra virgin olive oil

½ teaspoon sea salt

½ teaspoon black pepper

RANCH DRESSING

¾ cup raw cashew nuts, soaked in water for 2 hours, drained, and rinsed

1 tablespoon raw apple cider vinegar

½ cup raw coconut milk

1 garlic clove, crushed

½ teaspoon sea salt

2 scallions, finely chopped

2 tablespoons chopped fresh parsley

1. To make the dressing, put the soaked nuts, vinegar, ¼ cup of coconut milk, the garlic, and salt into a blender. Blend until you have a smooth paste. Add the rest of the coconut milk, a little at a time, until you have a fairly thick mix. It should be a cross between a dip and a pouring consistency. Stir in the scallions and parsley.

2. To make the salad, finely chop the vegetables and put them into a large serving bowl or smaller individual ones. Stir in all the remaining salad ingredients and serve.

You can vary the salad ingredients according to what you have or what is in season. For example, try swapping corn kernels for the yellow bell pepper.

PER SERVING : 360 CALS | 28.8G FAT | 7.2G SAT FAT | 22.7G CARBS | 9.4G SUGAR | 6G FIBER | 7.5G PROTEIN | 600MG SODIUM

SEAWEED & SESAME SALAD

SEAWEED IS A FANTASTIC SOURCE OF MINERALS AND FIBER—AND IF YOU CAN FIND A BAG OF MIXED SEAWEED, THE VARIETY OF COLORS AND TEXTURES IS A BEAUTIFUL SIGHT.

5 mins, plus soaking

None

2

1. While the seaweed is soaking, make the dressing. Add the sesame oil, rice vinegar, coconut aminos, chili, mirin, and miso paste to a small bowl and stir vigorously, to combine.

2. Once the seaweed is tender and reconstituted, drain it thoroughly in a colander and rinse.

3. Divide the seaweed between two shallow bowls and drizzle the dressing over it, tossing lightly.

4. Sprinkle the scallion and radish over the salad and garnish with the sesame seeds to serve.

INGREDIENTS

1 (¾-ounce) package mixed dried seaweed, soaked in water for 5–10 minutes

1 large scallion, finely chopped

1 red radish, finely chopped

2 teaspoons sesame seeds, to garnish

DRESSING

1 tablespoon cold-pressed extra virgin sesame oil

1 tablespoon raw rice vinegar

1 tablespoon raw coconut aminos sauce

1 teaspoon chopped red chile

2 teaspoons mirin

1 teaspoon organic miso paste

Dried seaweed mixes are widely available in health-food stores and online. Some kinds you can try are wakame, dulse, agar, miyoek, chondrus, gigartina, and kelp.

PER SERVING : 137 CALS | 9.2G FAT | 1.4G SAT FAT | 8.2G CARBS | 2.5G SUGAR | 1.1G FIBER | 11.6G PROTEIN | 200MG SODIUM

CAULIFLOWER SALAD WITH APPLE & NUTS

RAW CAULIFLOWER, WITH ITS MILD, SLIGHTLY NUTTY FLAVOR, TASTES WONDERFUL MIXED WITH CRISP SPIRALS OF APPLE, A SPRINKLING OF WALNUTS, AND A FABULOUS TANGY DRESSING.

INGREDIENTS

1 cauliflower, divided into small florets

1 large red-skinned dessert apple, such as Gala or McIntosh, cored and chopped

2 tablespoons sunflower seeds

1 tablespoon sesame seeds

3 tablespoons chopped raw walnuts

1 large sweet potato, peeled and spiralized

1 small red onion, spiralized

1 tablespoon cold-pressed extra virgin canola oil

½ teaspoon sea salt

¼ teaspoon black pepper

2 teaspoons chopped fresh dill, to garnish

DRESSING

3 tablespoons raw coconut yogurt

juice of ½ lemon

2 teaspoons grated fresh horseradish

1 tablespoon chopped fresh dill

1 garlic clove, crushed

½ teaspoon sea salt

½ teaspoon black pepper

1. Put the cauliflower florets into a large bowl. Add three-quarters of the apple, all of the seeds, and 2 tablespoons of the walnuts.

2. Beat all the dressing ingredients together in a small bowl and pour over the cauliflower mix. Stir well until everything is coated.

3. Divide the sweet potato spirals among four serving dishes and sprinkle the onion spirals on top. Drizzle with the canola oil, then add the salt and pepper.

4. Spoon the cauliflower mixture into the serving dishes. Top with the remaining apple and walnuts, and garnish with the dill to serve.

PER SERVING : 263 CALS | 14.2G FAT | 3.6G SAT FAT | 30.8G CARBS | 12.4G SUGAR | 7.5G FIBER | 7.1G PROTEIN | 680MG SODIUM

RAINBOW SALAD

MANGO, BELL PEPPERS, BLUEBERRIES, AND TOMATOES ARE ALL RICH IN ANTIOXIDANTS, AND NUTS AND SEEDS PROVIDE THE ESSENTIAL FATS NEEDED FOR HEALTHY CELL MEMBRANES.

INGREDIENTS

7 ounces halloumi cheese

2 cups arugula

1 mango, peeled, pitted, and chopped

12 cherry tomatoes, halved

1 yellow bell pepper, seeded and sliced

⅓ cup shredded snow peas

4 scallions, thinly sliced

⅓ cup blueberries

¼ cup sunflower seeds, toasted

¼ cup pumpkin seeds, toasted

¾ cup alfalfa sprouts

DRESSING

3 tablespoons olive oil

juice of 1 lemon

1 teaspoon honey

1 teaspoon mustard

1. To make the dressing, whisk together the oil, lemon juice, honey, and mustard.

2. Add the cheese to a dry skillet and cook for 3–4 minutes on each side, until golden.

3. Meanwhile, divide the arugula among four bowls, then top with the mango, tomatoes, yellow bell pepper, snow peas, scallions, and blueberries.

4. Top each serving with slices of cheese and sprinkle with the sunflower and pumpkin seeds and alfalfa sprouts.

5. Drizzle with the dressing and serve immediately.

The variations on this salad are endless. Use papaya instead of mango as an aid to digestion, or top the salad with broiled salmon or chicken for extra protein.

PER SERVING : 438 CALS | 32.9G FAT | 10.9G SAT FAT | 23.4G CARBS | 16.6G SUGAR | 4.8G FIBER | 17G PROTEIN | 400MG SODIUM

AVOCADO HERO SALAD

THIS SALAD IS FULL OF GORGEOUS TEXTURES, JUXTAPOSING CREAMY AVOCADO WITH CRUNCHY ASPARAGUS TIPS, AND IS RICH IN MONOUNSATURATED FATS, SOLUBLE FIBER, AND VITAMIN E.

10 mins, plus sprouting

None

INGREDIENTS

½ cup dry green peas suitable for sprouting

½ cup whole quinoa seeds suitable for sprouting

2½ cups baby spinach

2½ ounces baby asparagus tips

16 baby plum tomatoes

12 sprigs fresh watercress

2 ripe avocados, pitted, peeled, and sliced into bite-size pieces

2 tablespoons raw pine nuts

8 fresh basil sprigs

½ tablespoon cold-pressed extra virgin olive oil

DRESSING

2 tablespoons cold-pressed extra virgin olive oil

½ tablespoon raw wine vinegar

2 teaspoons raw honey

1 teaspoon stone-ground mustard

½ teaspoon sea salt

½ teaspoon pepper

1. To sprout the peas, put them in a wide glass jar and soak them overnight in lukewarm water, covered with cheesecloth or a similar material. In the morning, drain and rinse the peas and fill the jar with fresh water. Drain and rinse the peas twice a day for five days, until they sprout. Rinse and drain to use.

2. To sprout the quinoa, use the same method as the peas but soak them for only 4 hours. They will sprout in about two days.

3. Arrange the spinach, all but four of the asparagus tips, and the plum tomatoes in two serving dishes with most of the watercress.

4. Arrange three-quarters of the avocado slices in the dishes with the remaining watercress and the pea and quinoa sprouts. Sprinkle three-quarters of the pine nuts on top.

5. In a small bowl, mash the remaining avocado with the remaining pine nuts, six of the basil sprigs, and the ½ tablespoon of olive oil until you have a rough puree.

6. Make the dressing by thoroughly combining the ingredients in a small dish. Spoon most of it over the salad.

7. Finish the salad by arranging two asparagus tips in the center of each dish, followed by half the avocado puree and a basil sprig. Drizzle with the rest of the dressing to serve.

PER SERVING : 813 CALS | 48.5G FAT | 6.2G SAT FAT | 80.6G CARBS | 13.3G SUGAR | 27.1G FIBER | 23.4G PROTEIN | 1.6G SODIUM

GADO GADO SALAD

TOSSING CAULIFLOWER AND BROCCOLI WITH BEAN SPROUTS AND CUCUMBER AND ADDING A TOASTED PEANUT AND SOY DRESSING TURNS EVERYDAY INGREDIENTS INTO SOMETHING EXOTIC.

10–15 mins | 7–8 mins | 4

INGREDIENTS

½ small head cauliflower, cored and cut into small florets

1½ cups small broccoli florets

1½ cups shredded savoy cabbage

1½ cups bean sprouts

1 cucumber, peeled, halved lengthwise, seeded, and thickly sliced

1 red bell pepper, halved, seeded, and finely chopped

DRESSING

2 tablespoons peanut oil

½ cup unsalted peanuts, finely chopped

2 garlic cloves, finely chopped

2 tablespoons gluten-free soy sauce

juice of 2 limes

½ red chile, seeded and finely chopped

1. Put the cauliflower, broccoli, cabbage, bean sprouts, cucumber, and red bell pepper into a salad bowl and toss gently together.

2. To make the dressing, heat 1 tablespoon of the oil in a skillet over medium heat. Add the peanuts and garlic and stir-fry for 2–3 minutes, or until lightly browned. Remove from the heat and stir in the soy sauce, lime juice, chile, and remaining oil, then let cool.

3. When ready to eat, spoon the dressing over the salad and toss gently together. Spoon into four bowls, then serve immediately.

Popular in Chinese and Asian recipes, mung bean sprouts are widely available in supermarkets all year round. Low in calories, they can be added to salads in place of noodles or rice.

PER SERVING : 259 CALS | 17.8G FAT | 2.6G SAT FAT | 20.4G CARBS | 8.2G SUGAR | 6.6G FIBER | 10.8G PROTEIN | 480MG SODIUM

CUCUMBER NOODLE BOWL WITH THAI DRESSING

THIS SPICY THAI SALAD IS FULL OF CHOLESTEROL-LOWERING FOODS, SUCH AS BEETS, KALE, AND SEAWEED. IT ALSO FEATURES A YUMMY PEANUT TOPPING FOR A HEALTHY HEART.

INGREDIENTS

1 beet, peeled and spiralized

½ cucumber, spiralized

1 cup chopped kale

½ red onion, thinly sliced

1 small carrot, peeled and thinly sliced

⅓ cup raw peanuts

2 teaspoons ground red seaweed

¼ cup fresh coconut flakes, to garnish

1 tablespoon fresh cilantro leaves, to garnish

DRESSING

2 tablespoons cold-pressed extra virgin sesame oil

2 teaspoons organic miso paste

juice of ½ lime

½-inch piece of fresh ginger, minced

1 large garlic clove, minced

1 small red chile, minced

2 teaspoons raw peanut butter

salt (optional)

1. Arrange all but a few strands of the beet in two serving bowls. Add all of the cucumber strands.

2. Add the kale to the bowls and top with the onion and carrot.

3. To make the dressing, combine all the ingredients in a small bowl and mix well. Spoon it over the beet salad.

4. Run the peanuts under cold water, then pat dry so they are just slightly damp. On a plate, roll them in the seaweed until thoroughly coated, then sprinkle them over the salad.

5. Add the coconut flakes and cilantro leaves to the salad. Garnish with the remaining beet strands to serve.

You can use raw almond butter or raw cashew butter in the dressing and you can choose either of these nuts for the garnish.

PER SERVING : 409 CALS | 30.4G FAT | 6.7G SAT FAT | 29.1G CARBS | 12.1G SUGAR | 8.4G FIBER | 11.5G PROTEIN | 280MG SODIUM

SALMON & EDAMAME SALAD

SALMON IS A REAL SUPERFOOD—NOT ONLY DELICIOUS, BUT RICH IN PROTEIN AND OMEGA-3 FATS, WHICH ARE IMPORTANT FOR PHYSICAL AND MENTAL HEALTH.

INGREDIENTS

14 ounces salmon fillets

1⅓ cups frozen edamame, thawed

1⅓ cups frozen peas, thawed

½ cup roasted red pepper strips

2 cups fresh arugula

⅓ cup fresh dill, chopped

pepper (optional)

DRESSING

3 tablespoons olive oil

1½ tablespoons lemon juice

1 teaspoon whole-grain mustard

1 teaspoon honey

1. Preheat the broiler. For the dressing, whisk the olive oil, lemon juice, mustard, and honey together in a small bowl. Set aside.

2. Broil the salmon fillets under a medium heat for 3–4 minutes on each side, until the fish is opaque and flaky when separated with a fork. Break into large flakes.

3. Meanwhile, bring a large saucepan of water to a boil and add the edamame soybeans and peas to the water. Cook for 3–4 minutes, until just tender. Drain and run under cold water to refresh.

4. Place the salmon flakes, beans, peas, red pepper strips, arugula, and dill in a large bowl. Pour the dressing over the top and season with pepper, if using. Toss well to combine. Divide among four bowls and serve.

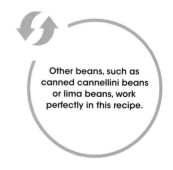

Other beans, such as canned cannellini beans or lima beans, work perfectly in this recipe.

PER SERVING : 446 CALS | 30.3G FAT | 5.2G SAT FAT | 13G CARBS | 5.8G SUGAR | 5.1G FIBER | 29.9G PROTEIN | 120MG SODIUM

HARISSA CHICKEN SALAD

CAPTURE THE FLAVORS OF MOROCCO WITH THIS SPICY BROWN RICE SALAD, FLECKED WITH DICED DRIED APRICOTS AND GLISTENING RAISINS AND TOSSED WITH GREEN KALE.

10–15 mins · 40–48 mins · 4

INGREDIENTS

1⅓ cups easy-cook brown rice

2 teaspoons tomato paste

1 pound 2 ounces skinless chicken breasts

½ cup diced dried apricots

⅓ cup raisins

½ preserved lemon, drained and finely chopped

1 small red onion, finely chopped

1¼ cups shredded kale

3 tablespoons pine nuts, toasted

DRESSING

2 teaspoons harissa

¼ cup olive oil

juice of 1 lemon

salt and pepper (optional)

1. Put the rice into a saucepan of boiling water. Bring back to a boil, then simmer for 25–30 minutes, or until tender. Drain, then transfer to a salad bowl.

2. Put the harissa, oil, and lemon juice in a lidded jar, season with salt and pepper, if using, screw on the lid, and shake well.

3. Spoon 2 tablespoons of the dressing into a bowl and mix in the tomato paste. Preheat the broiler to high and line the broiler pan with foil. Put the chicken on the foil. Brush some of the tomato dressing over the chicken, then broil for 15–18 minutes, turning the meat and brushing it with the remaining tomato dressing halfway through. Cut through a breast to check that the meat is no longer pink and any juices run clear. Cover and let cool.

4. Drizzle the rest of the dressing over the rice. Add the apricots, raisins, lemon, and onion, then toss together and let cool.

5. Add the kale and pine nuts to the salad and stir well. Thinly slice the chicken, arrange it over the salad, and serve.

PER SERVING : 668 CALS | 24G FAT | 3.1G SAT FAT | 78.8G CARBS | 22.1G SUGAR | 6.4G FIBER | 36.3G PROTEIN | 360MG SODIUM

BROILED CHICKEN & SLAW BOWL

HERE'S A PERFECT MIDWEEK MEAL FOR ESSENTIAL PROTEIN AND ENERGY: CRUNCHY VEGETABLES DRIZZLED IN A SPICY MAYONNAISE AND TOPPED WITH TENDER SLICES OF CHICKEN.

INGREDIENTS

4 (5½-ounce) boneless, skinless chicken breasts

1 teaspoon smoked paprika

salt and pepper (optional)

12 fresh arugula leaves, to garnish

COLESLAW

2 carrots, peeled and grated

1 fennel bulb, trimmed and thinly sliced

1 beet, grated

1½ cups shredded red cabbage

1½ cups shredded green cabbage

4 radishes, thinly sliced

1 red onion, peeled and thinly sliced

⅓ cup mixed herbs, such as parsley, dill, mint, and cilantro, chopped

juice of 1 lemon

2 tablespoons extra virgin olive oil

1 cup plain yogurt

1 tablespoon gluten-free whole-grain mustard

1. To make the coleslaw, put all the coleslaw ingredients together into a large bowl. Toss together really well and set aside.

2. Preheat the broiler to a medium heat. Place the chicken breasts between two sheets of wax paper and flatten with a rolling pin or mallet, to a thickness of ½–¾ inch.

3. Season the chicken with paprika, and salt and pepper, if using. Broil for 4–5 minutes on each side, until the chicken is tender and the juices run clear when the tip of a sharp knife is inserted into the thickest part of the meat.

4. Divide the coleslaw among four bowls and top with slices of chicken breast and the arugula leaves.

Flattening the chicken breasts helps the chicken to cook more quickly and evenly. Remove the skin, because this is where the fat is.

PER SERVING : 362 CALS | 13.4G FAT | 3.1G SAT FAT | 21.9G CARBS | 12.7G SUGAR | 6.1G FIBER | 39.2G PROTEIN | 200MG SODIUM

TURKEY WALDORF BOWL

THIS TURKEY SALAD, PAIRED WITH LOADS OF CRUNCHY RAW FRUIT
AND VEGETABLES AND TAHINI AND LIME DRESSING, IS HARD TO BEAT.

INGREDIENTS

2½ cups shredded cooked turkey

2 celery stalks, thinly sliced

½ cup shredded red cabbage

2 crisp apples, cored and chopped

⅔ cup seedless red grapes, halved

1 cup shredded savoy cabbage

¾ cup walnuts, toasted

½ cup pecans, toasted

DRESSING

3 tablespoons gluten-free tahini

2 tablespoons lime juice

2 teaspoons agave syrup

1 teaspoon soy sauce

salt and pepper (optional)

1. Whisk together the tahini, lime juice, agave syrup, and soy sauce and season with salt and pepper, if using.

2. Lightly toss together the remaining ingredients, then toss again with the dressing. Divide among four large, shallow bowls and serve immediately.

You can use chicken or even smoked mackerel in place of turkey in this salad. If using mackerel, add a little creamed horseradish to the dressing for a real kick.

PER SERVING : 482 CALS | 29.3G FAT | 3.4G SAT FAT | 29.1G CARBS | 17.4G SUGAR | 6.8G FIBER | 32.8G PROTEIN | 200MG SODIUM

MAIN DISHES

HARISSA VEGGIE BOWL

THIS VEGGIE BOWL INCLUDES HOMEMADE HUMMUS MADE WITH ROASTED CARROTS—
HOWEVER, YOU COULD REPLACE THE CARROTS WITH TOASTED WALNUTS OR AVOCADO.

INGREDIENTS

1 red bell pepper, seeded and
cut into wedges

1 yellow bell pepper, seeded and
cut into wedges

6 ounces baby broccoli

1 large red onion, peeled and
cut into wedges

2 teaspoons gluten-free harissa paste

¼ cup hazelnuts

⅓ cup crumbled feta cheese (optional)

HUMMUS

8 carrots, peeled and thickly sliced

¼ teaspoon cumin seeds

3 tablespoons olive oil

1½ cups drained and rinsed,
canned chickpeas

1 garlic clove, coarsely chopped

1 tablespoon tahini

juice of 1 small lemon

salt and pepper (optional)

1. Preheat the oven to 400°F.

2. To make the hummus, put the carrots into a roasting pan and sprinkle with the cumin seeds and ½ tablespoon of the oil. Roast in the preheated oven for 20–25 minutes, until tender.

3. Meanwhile, arrange the remaining vegetables in a single layer in a separate large roasting pan. Mix the harissa paste with 1 tablespoon of the oil and sprinkle it over the vegetables, then roast for 35 minutes. Add the hazelnuts after 20 minutes of cooking.

4. Place the cooked carrots in a food processor with the chickpeas and garlic and process until broken down. Add the tahini and lemon juice and process again until nearly smooth. Add the remaining oil, season with salt and pepper, if using, and process for the final time.

5. Divide the hummus among four warm bowls, then top with the roasted vegetables and hazelnuts and sprinkle with the cheese, if using.

PER SERVING : 327 CALS | 20.7G FAT | 2.3G SAT FAT | 28.3G CARBS | 10.3G SUGAR | 9.4G FIBER | 8.6G PROTEIN | 120MG SODIUM

WINTER BLISS BOWL

A HEALTHY, CRUNCHY MAIN DISH THAT IS FILLING AND FULL OF FIBER FOR A HEALTHY DIGESTION. THIS IS THE PERFECT WAY TO "EAT A RAINBOW," WITH A SPICY, HIGH-PROTEIN FALAFEL.

INGREDIENTS

2⅓ cups shredded green cabbage

2⅓ cups shredded red cabbage

1 small red bell pepper, seeded and finely sliced

1 celery stalk, finely sliced

1 carrot, peeled and grated

1½ tablespoons pomegranate seeds

2½ tablespoons coarsely chopped walnuts

1 tablespoon coarsely chopped fresh parsley

LEMON DRESSING

2 tablespoons plain yogurt

juice of 1 lemon

1 teaspoon Dijon mustard

PATTIES

1½ cups drained and rinsed, canned chickpeas

1 teaspoon harissa paste

1 tablespoon all-purpose flour

½ teaspoon ground cumin

¼ cup fresh cilantro

1 tablespoon olive oil

salt and pepper (optional)

1. Put the green cabbage and red cabbage into a large bowl with the red bell pepper, celery, carrot, half the pomegranate seeds, and half the walnuts, and mix well to combine.

2. To make the lemon dressing, whisk together the yogurt, half the lemon juice, and the mustard. Season with salt and pepper, if using, and mix into the shredded vegetables.

3. To make the patties, put the chickpeas into a food processor along with the harissa paste, flour, cumin, cilantro, and the remaining lemon juice. Season with salt and pepper, if using, and process until smooth.

4. Shape the mixture into eight patties.

5. Heat the oil in a skillet, then add the patties and cook for 3–4 minutes on each side, until golden.

6. Serve the patties with the colorful slaw, sprinkled with the remaining pomegranate seeds and walnuts and the parsley.

PER SERVING : 212 CALS | 8.8G FAT | 1.1G SAT FAT | 26.5G CARBS | 13.3G SUGAR | 8.3G FIBER | 7.3G PROTEIN | 80MG SODIUM

MAPLE TOFU WITH EGG-FRIED RICE

TOFU IS A GREAT SOURCE OF VEGETARIAN PROTEIN, AND IS A VERSATILE INGREDIENT—IT CAN BE MARINATED BEFORE COOKING OR COOKED, AS HERE, IN A TASTY MAPLE SAUCE.

INGREDIENTS

1 egg

2 teaspoons sesame oil

3 tablespoons coconut oil

1⅓ cups cooked long-grain rice

½ teaspoon ground turmeric

⅔ cup frozen peas, thawed

4 scallions, finely chopped

1 cup bean sprouts

⅓ cup cashew nuts

11¾ ounces tofu, drained and dried on paper towels

3 bok choy, quartered lengthwise

2 tablespoons sesame seeds, toasted

MAPLE SAUCE

3 garlic cloves, crushed

3 tablespoons gluten-free soy sauce

2 tablespoons maple syrup

1 tablespoon rice vinegar

1. Beat together the egg and sesame oil and set aside. Heat 2 tablespoons of the coconut oil in a wok or large skillet, add the rice and turmeric, and stir-fry for 3–4 minutes.

2. Add the peas, scallions, bean sprouts, and cashew nuts and stir-fry for 3 minutes.

3. Push the rice to one side of the wok, pour in the egg mixture, and let set for a few seconds, then move it around with chopsticks to break it up. Stir into the rice, then remove from the heat and cover while you cook the tofu.

4. Heat the remaining coconut oil in a skillet, add the tofu, and cook for 4–5 minutes, turning frequently, until lightly browned.

5. Mix the garlic, soy sauce, maple syrup, and vinegar together, add to the tofu, and cook, stirring occasionally, for 2–3 minutes, until the sauce thickens. Meanwhile, steam the bok choy.

6. Divide the rice among four warm bowls, top with the bok choy and maple tofu, sprinkle with the sesame seeds, and serve immediately.

PER SERVING : 614 CALS | 29.4G FAT | 11.9G SAT FAT | 63.8G CARBS | 11.5G SUGAR | 6.87G FIBER | 27G PROTEIN | 760MG SODIUM

SWEET ROOTS BOWL

FULL OF STARCH AND SUGAR, ROOT VEGETABLES GIVE YOUR ENERGY LEVELS A LONG-TERM BOOST.
USING TAHINI IN DRESSINGS INCREASES YOUR INTAKE OF PROTEIN AND ESSENTIAL FATS.

INGREDIENTS

2 sweet potatoes, cut into chunks

2 beets, cut into chunks

2 red onions, cut into wedges

2 tablespoons olive oil

2 teaspoons cumin seeds

½ cup brown rice

3 cups shredded kale

2 tablespoons slivered almonds, toasted

TAHINI DRESSING

¼ cup gluten-free tahini

juice of 1 lemon

½ teaspoon pepper

½ teaspoon honey

1. Preheat the oven to 400°F.

2. Put the sweet potatoes, beets, and onions into a bowl with the oil and cumin seeds and toss together to coat with the oil.

3. Transfer to a roasting pan and roast in the preheated oven for 35–40 minutes, until tender.

4. Meanwhile, cook the rice according to the package directions.

5. To make the dressing, whisk together the tahini, lemon juice, pepper, and honey.

6. Stir the kale into the root vegetables 10 minutes before the end of the roasting time.

7. Drain the rice and divide among four warm bowls.

8. Toss the vegetables with the dressing and serve on top of the rice, sprinkled with the toasted almonds.

PER SERVING : 402 CALS | 18.4G FAT | 2.3G SAT FAT | 54.2G CARBS | 11.8G SUGAR | 9.5G FIBER | 10.1G PROTEIN | 120MG SODIUM

VEGGIE BURGER BOWL

THESE BURGERS ARE FILLING AND NUTRITIOUS—YOU COULD EAT THEM IN A BUN, BUT SERVING THEM IN A BOWL ON A BED OF COLORFUL ROASTED RATATOUILLE IS JUST AS DELICIOUS.

25 mins, plus chilling | 35–40 mins | 4

INGREDIENTS

2 red bell peppers, seeded and chopped

2 yellow bell peppers, seeded and chopped

2 red onions, cut into wedges

2 zucchini, thickly sliced

3 tablespoons olive oil

1½ cups drained and rinsed, canned chickpeas

1⅓ cups frozen peas, thawed

1⅓ cups frozen corn kernels, thawed

⅓ cup fresh cilantro (including stems)

¼ teaspoon cumin

⅔ cup all-purpose flour

1 tablespoon sunflower seeds

1 tablespoon sesame seeds

salt and pepper (optional)

DRESSING

1 avocado, peeled, pitted, and chopped

¾ cup plain yogurt

2 scallions, chopped

1 garlic clove, crushed

1 tablespoon lime juice

salt and pepper (optional)

1. Preheat the oven to 400°F. Put the red bell peppers, yellow bell peppers, onions, and zucchini into a roasting pan and drizzle with 1 tablespoon of the oil. Roast for 35–40 minutes, until they are slightly charred at the edges.

2. Meanwhile, put the chickpeas, peas, corn, cilantro, cumin, and ½ cup of the flour into a food processor and process to a thick paste. Add the sunflower seeds and sesame seeds, season with salt and pepper, if using, and process again to mix together.

3. Using wet hands, divide the mixture into four portions and shape each portion into a patty. Dust the patties with the remaining flour and chill in the refrigerator for 20 minutes.

4. Meanwhile to make the dressing, put the avocado, yogurt, scallions, garlic, and lime juice into a small blender and blend until smooth. Season with salt and pepper, if using.

5. Heat the remaining oil in a skillet, add the patties, and cook for 5–6 minutes on each side, until cooked through.

6. Divide the ratatouille among four bowls, top each one with a burger, then drizzle with the dressing and serve immediately.

PER SERVING : 534 CALS | 24G FAT | 4G SAT FAT | 66G CARBS | 18.6G SUGAR | 15.8G FIBER | 16.9G PROTEIN | 40MG SODIUM

SWEET & SOUR "STIR-FRY"

THIS ASIAN-INSPIRED BOWL IS FILLED WITH GOODIES—RAW KELP NOODLES ARE LOW IN CARBS AND CALORIES, AND ASIAN MUSHROOMS CAN HELP REGULATE THE IMMUNE SYSTEM.

15 mins, plus sprouting and soaking

20–25 mins

2

INGREDIENTS

¼ cup adzuki beans suitable for sprouting

3 tabllespoons mung beans suitable for sprouting

1 parsnip, peeled and coarsely chopped

1 small sweet potato, peeled and coarsely chopped

1½ tablespoons dried shiitake mushrooms, soaked in water for 15 minutes, drained, and rinsed

7 ounces raw kelp noodles

¾ cup sliced bok choy

1¾ ounces enoki mushrooms

1 mild red chile, seeded and finely sliced

¼ cup raw pine nuts

CHILI SAUCE

1 small, medium–hot red chile, seeded and chopped

1 teaspoon peeled and chopped fresh ginger

1 tablespoon raw coconut aminos sauce

2 teaspoons raw agave nectar

1 tablespoon cold-pressed extra virgin sesame oil

1 teaspoon raw tahini

juice of ½ lime

2 teaspoons raw rice vinegar

1. Start sprouting the adzuki and mung beans three days before making the stir-fry. Put the beans in a wide glass jar and soak them overnight in lukewarm water, covered with cheesecloth or a similar material. In the morning, drain and rinse the beans and fill the jar with fresh water. Drain and rinse them twice a day for three days, until they have sprouted. Rinse and drain to use.

2. For the sauce, process all the ingredients to create a paste. Add water until you have a thick pouring consistency and stir well.

3. Put the parsnip into a food processor and process until you have rice-size pieces. Transfer to a mixing bowl. Do the same with the sweet potato and then lightly mix the two vegetables.

4. Chop the soaked shiitake mushrooms into small pieces and mix them into the vegetable rice.

5. Rinse the kelp noodles and shake to dry in a strainer. Arrange most of them in two serving bowls and add the vegetable rice.

6. Arrange the bok choy and enoki mushrooms on top of the rice, then dot spoonfuls of the sauce around the dish. Finish with the chile slices, pine nuts, and bean sprouts. Finally, arrange the remaining kelp noodles on top and serve.

PER SERVING : 489 CALS | 19.2G FAT | 2G SAT FAT | 69.2G CARBS | 14.8G SUGAR | 14.1G FIBER | 12.5G PROTEIN | 120MG SODIUM

BLACK RICE & POMEGRANATE BOWL

THIS COLORFUL BOWL IS BURSTING WITH PROTEIN-RICH LIMA BEANS, BLACK RICE, AND COTTAGE CHEESE. FULL OF GOODNESS, IT WILL HELP SUSTAIN YOUR ENERGY LEVELS.

INGREDIENTS

1 small butternut squash, seeded and diced

1 red onion, peeled and sliced

1 tablespoon olive oil

⅔ cup black rice

1 cup shredded kale

2 tablespoons pine nuts

1½ cups drained and rinsed, canned lima beans

¼ cup cottage cheese, to serve

seeds from 1 pomegranate, to serve

TAHINI DRESSING

¼ cup gluten-free tahini paste

juice of 1 lemon

1 garlic clove, crushed

2 tablespoons extra virgin olive oil

1. Preheat the oven to 400°F.

2. Put the butternut squash and onion into a roasting pan and drizzle with the olive oil. Roast in the preheated oven for 15 minutes.

3. Cook the rice according to the package directions.

4. Meanwhile, add the kale and pine nuts to the squash and roast for an additional 10 minutes. Remove from the oven and toss in the lima beans.

5. To make the dressing, whisk the tahini, lemon juice, garlic, and olive oil together in a small bowl. Set aside.

6. Drain the rice and divide among four warm bowls. Spoon the roasted vegetables and nuts over the rice, and add a dollop of cottage cheese and a sprinkling of pomegranate seeds.

7. Drizzle the dressing into each bowl to serve.

PER SERVING : 492 CALS | 23.7G FAT | 3.3G SAT FAT | 58.7G CARBS | 10.7G SUGAR | 10.5G FIBER | 14.8G PROTEIN | 80MG SODIUM

LENTIL & AMARANTH TABBOULEH

AMARANTH IS A HIGH-QUALITY SOURCE OF PLANT PROTEIN. IT'S ALSO BURSTING WITH IRON AND CALCIUM, SO IT'S AN ESSENTIAL GRAIN TO HAVE IN YOUR KITCHEN.

25 mins · 30 mins · 4

INGREDIENTS

¾ cup amaranth

2 cups drained and rinsed, canned green lentils or cooked green lentils

½ cucumber, diced

8 tomatoes, diced

1 small red onion, peeled and diced

⅓ cup fresh parsley, chopped

⅓ cup fresh mint, chopped

⅓ cup fresh cilantro, chopped

¾ cup hazelnuts, toasted and chopped

5½ ounces halloumi cheese, thickly sliced

salt and pepper (optional)

seeds from 1 pomegranate, to garnish

2 tablespoons coconut flakes, to garnish

2 tablespoons avocado oil, to serve

DRESSING

3 tablespoons olive oil

1 tablespoon balsamic vinegar

1 teaspoon whole-grain mustard

1 teaspoon honey

1. Cook the amaranth according to the package directions, until the grains are fluffy. Drain and let cool for a few minutes.

2. Meanwhile, make the dressing. Whisk the olive oil, vinegar, mustard, and honey together in a bowl.

3. Put the amaranth into a large bowl with the lentils, cucumber, tomatoes, onion, herbs, and hazelnuts. Pour the dressing over the top and toss together. Season with salt and pepper, if using, and let stand at room temperature.

4. In a dry skillet, cook the halloumi over medium heat until golden on both sides.

5. Serve the halloumi with the tabbouleh, garnished with pomegranate seeds, coconut flakes, and a drizzle of avocado oil.

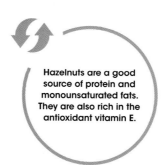

Hazelnuts are a good source of protein and monounsaturated fats. They are also rich in the antioxidant vitamin E.

PER SERVING : 727 CALS | 47.1G FAT | 10.9G SAT FAT | 57.8G CARBS | 17.1G SUGAR | 12.8G FIBER | 23.5G PROTEIN | 480MG SODIUM

QUINOA CHILI

QUINOA IS A SOUTH AMERICAN GRAIN THAT CONTAINS ALL NINE ESSENTIAL AMINO ACIDS. IT'S EASY TO COOK AND IS A GREAT, WHEAT-FREE REPLACEMENT FOR RICE OR COUSCOUS.

INGREDIENTS

¼ cup red quinoa

1 tablespoon olive oil, for sautéing

1 onion, peeled and diced

2 green chiles, seeded and diced

1½ teaspoons smoked paprika

1 teaspoon chili powder

2 teaspoons cumin powder

½ teaspoon cayenne pepper

2 garlic cloves, crushed

3⅓ cups canned diced tomatoes

1½ cups drained and rinsed, canned kidney beans

1½ cups drained and rinsed, canned great northern beans

½ cup water

⅓ cup chopped fresh cilantro leaves

2 tablespoons frozen corn kernels, thawed

2 tablespoons sour cream, to serve

1. Cook the quinoa according to the package directions.

2. Meanwhile, heat the oil in a separate large saucepan and sauté the onion over medium heat for 3–4 minutes to soften.

3. Add the chiles to the pan and cook for 1 minute. Stir in the spices and garlic, and cook for an additional 1 minute.

4. Drain the quinoa and add to the pan along with the tomatoes, beans, and water. Bring to a simmer and cook for 30 minutes, stirring occasionally, until thickened. Stir in half the cilantro leaves.

5. Divide the chili among four warm serving bowls and sprinkle the corn kernels and remaining cilantro over the top. Serve with the sour cream.

An average portion of kidney beans contains at least one-quarter of our day's iron needs to help prevent anemia and increase energy levels.

PER SERVING : 277 CALS | 7.4G FAT | 1.3G SAT FAT | 38.6G CARBS | 10.5G SUGAR | 9.6G FIBER | 12.3G PROTEIN | 40MG SODIUM

ROASTED CAULIFLOWER, KALE & CHICKPEA BOWL

THE SPICES IN THIS VEGGIE-PACKED BOWL ALL HAVE HEALTH PROPERTIES—GINGER IS SEEN AS A CURE-ALL, TURMERIC IS AN ANTI-INFLAMMATORY, AND CINNAMON HELPS STABILISE BLOOD SUGAR.

INGREDIENTS

1 teaspoon ground turmeric

1 teaspoon mustard seeds

½ teaspoon cumin seeds

½ teaspoon ground ginger

½ teaspoon ground coriander

½ teaspoon ground cinnamon

1 head of cauliflower, broken into florets

1½ cups drained and rinsed, canned chickpeas

2 red onions, thickly sliced

2 tablespoons olive oil

3 cups shredded kale

2 cups fresh whole-wheat bread crumbs

3 tablespoons walnuts, chopped

2 tablespoons slivered almonds

⅔ cup freshly grated Parmesan cheese

1. Preheat the oven to 400°F.

2. Dry-fry the turmeric, mustard seeds, cumin seeds, ginger, coriander, and cinnamon in a small skillet for 2 minutes, or until the mustard seeds start to "pop."

3. Put the cauliflower florets, chickpeas, and onion slices into a large roasting pan. Sprinkle with the spices and toss well together.

4. Drizzle the oil over the top and toss again.

5. Roast in the preheated oven for 20 minutes.

6. Stir the kale into the roasted vegetables, and roast for an additional 10 minutes, until the vegetables are tender and slightly charred.

7. Mix the bread crumbs, walnuts, almonds, and grated cheese together and sprinkle the mixture over the vegetables. Roast for an additional 5–8 minutes, until they are golden.

8. Divide among four bowls and serve immediately.

PER SERVING : 406 CALS | 19.5G FAT | 4.2G SAT FAT | 41.4G CARBS | 10.7G SUGAR | 12.2G FIBER | 19.5G PROTEIN | 360MG SODIUM

KIMCHI TOFU BOWL

KIMCHI IS A KOREAN PICKLE, USED TO ADD A SOUR, TANGY FLAVOR TO FOOD—IT IS SAID TO BE GOOD FOR DIGESTION AND ALL-ROUND HEALTH.

20 mins, plus marinating

43–55 mins

4

INGREDIENTS

⅓ cup brown rice

⅓ cup Camargue red rice or extra brown rice

⅓ cup wild rice

3 cups cold water

3 tablespoons mirin

1 teaspoon gluten-free soy sauce

2 tablespoons miso paste

7 ounces tofu, cut into triangles

1 tablespoon coconut oil

2 red bell peppers, seeded and sliced

4 scallions, trimmed and sliced

2 zucchini, cut into matchsticks

1 carrot, cut into matchsticks

2½ ounces shiitake mushrooms, sliced

½ cup edamame soybeans

½ cup bean sprouts

¼ cup kimchi

1. Rinse the rice thoroughly. Put into a saucepan with the water. Bring to a boil, then cover and simmer gently for 20–25 minutes, or according to package directions, until cooked.

2. Meanwhile, mix the mirin, soy sauce, and miso paste together and put into a nonmetallic bowl. Add the tofu triangles, turning to coat with the marinade, then let marinate for 15–20 minutes.

3. Heat the coconut oil in a wok or large skillet, add the red bell peppers and scallions, and stir-fry for 2–3 minutes, then add the zucchini and carrot and stir-fry for an additional 3–4 minutes.

4. Add the mushrooms, edamame soybeans, bean sprouts, tofu, and marinade. Stir-fry for 1 minute, then cover and steam for 2 minutes.

5. Drain the rice and divide among four warm bowls. Top each portion with the stir-fry and 1 tablespoon of kimchi.

This recipe includes tofu, a good source of vegetarian protein, but you could use strips of chicken or shrimp if you like.

PER SERVING : 423 CALS | 11.4G FAT | 4.3G SAT FAT | 59.4G CARBS | 110G SUGAR | 8.7G FIBER | 18.8G PROTEIN | 480MG SODIUM

PROTEIN RICE BOWL

BROWN RICE ADDS IMPORTANT FIBER AND FRESH CHILE SUPPLIES SOME
HEAT TO THIS PROTEIN-RICH VEGETARIAN LUNCH FOR TWO.

INGREDIENTS

¾ cup brown rice
2 extra-large eggs
2½ cups spinach
4 scallions, finely chopped
1 red chile, seeded and finely sliced
½ ripe avocado, sliced
2 tablespoons roasted peanuts

VINAIGRETTE

2 tablespoons olive oil
1 teaspoon Dijon mustard
1 tablespoon apple cider vinegar
juice of ½ lemon

1. Put the rice into a large saucepan and cover with twice the volume of water. Bring to a boil and simmer for 25 minutes, or according to package directions, until the rice is tender and the liquid has nearly all disappeared. Continue to simmer for an additional few minutes if some liquid remains.

2. Meanwhile, cook the eggs. Bring a small saucepan of water to a boil. Carefully add the eggs to the pan and boil for 7 minutes—the whites will be cooked and the yolks should still be slightly soft. Drain and pour cold water over the eggs to stop them from cooking. When cool enough to handle, tap them on the work surface to crack the shells and peel them. Cut the eggs into quarters.

3. Stir the spinach, half of the scallions, and a little red chile into the cooked rice.

4. To make the vinaigrette, whisk the olive oil, Dijon mustard, cider vinegar, and lemon juice together. Pour the dressing over the warm rice and mix to combine.

5. Divide the rice between two bowls and top each with the remaining scallions, avocado, remaining red chile, peanuts, and egg quarters.

PER SERVING : 653 CALS | 33.9G FAT | 5.9G SAT FAT | 71.1G CARBS | 4G SUGAR | 8.7G FIBER | 19.1G PROTEIN | 120MG SODIUM

SESAME SHRIMP WITH WATERMELON BOWL

THIS UNUSUAL COMBINATION REALLY DOES TASTE DELICIOUS—SUCCULENT, CRISP WATERMELON WITH RICH SHRIMP AND A CITRUS DRESSING. PERFECT FOR A SUMMER'S DAY.

12 mins · None · 2

INGREDIENTS

3 tablespoons extra virgin olive oil

juice of 1 lime

1 garlic clove, crushed

1/10 watermelon (about 1¼ pounds), peeled, seeded, and sliced

16 sprigs watercress

7 ounces cooked jumbo shrimp

⅓ cup cashew nuts, toasted

2 scallions, sliced

1 red chile, sliced

2 teaspoons black sesame seeds

1. To make the dressing whisk together the oil, lime juice, and garlic in a small bowl.

2. Divide the watermelon, watercress, shrimp, nuts, scallions, chille, and sesame seeds between two bowls.

3. Drizzle with the dressing to serve.

For a winter variation of this recipe, try roasting slices of butternut squash to replace the watermelon—both are rich in great nutrients due to their vibrant color.

PER SERVING : 544 CALS | 34.1G FAT | 5.4G SAT FAT | 35.5G CARBS | 20.2G SUGAR | 3.2G FIBER | 31G PROTEIN | 120MG SODIUM

SALMON BURRITO BOWL

SALMON IS A GREAT SOURCE OF ESSENTIAL FATS AND PROTEIN. SERVED HERE WITH RICE AND BEANS, THIS RECIPE ADDS A REAL PROTEIN BOOST TO YOUR DAY.

INGREDIENTS

SALMON

1 tablespoon coconut oil

2 garlic cloves, crushed

1 red onion, peeled and diced

1 celery stalk, diced

1 red bell pepper, seeded and diced

1½ cups drained and rinsed, canned red kidney beans

1 cup long-grain rice

2½ cups vegetable broth

2 tablespoons jerk paste

2 tablespoons honey

4 salmon fillets, each weighing 5½ ounces

MANGO SALSA

1 large mango, peeled, pitted, and diced

½ red onion, finely diced

2 tablespoons chopped fresh cilantro

juice of 1 lime

1. To make the mango salsa, mix the mango, onion, cilantro, and lime juice together and let stand at room temperature.

2. Meanwhile, heat the coconut oil in a large saucepan, add the garlic, onion, celery, and red bell pepper, and sauté for 4–5 minutes. Add the kidney beans to the pan.

3. Add the rice and broth, bring to a boil, cover, and simmer for about 15 minutes, or according to package directions, until the rice is tender and the liquid has been absorbed.

4. Meanwhile, mix together the jerk paste and honey. Preheat the broiler to hot and line a broiler pan with foil. Place the salmon fillets on the prepared pan and spread the jerk mixture over each one.

5. Cook the salmon under the broiler for 8–10 minutes, turning once.

6. Serve the rice in warm bowls, topped with a fillet of salmon and some mango salsa.

If you can't get salmon, try using a white fish, such as cod or halibut—both work well in this recipe.

PER SERVING : 716 CALS | 26.2G FAT | 8.4G SAT FAT | 78G CARBS | 23.7G SUGAR | 7.7G FIBER | 40.3G PROTEIN | 760MG SODIUM

ONE-PAN SPICY CHICKEN

THIS DISH IS BASED ON THE GORGEOUS STEWS MADE IN MOROCCO, USING APRICOTS TO ADD SWEETNESS AND A COMBINATION OF SPICES FOR A FRAGRANT SAUCE.

15 mins | 30–35 mins | 4

INGREDIENTS

2 onions, peeled, 1 chopped and 1 sliced

1 small–medium tomato, halved

1¼-inch piece fresh ginger, peeled and chopped

3 garlic cloves, peeled

2 tablespoons olive oil

4 (5½-ounce) boneless, skinless chicken breasts, cut into bite-size pieces

2 teaspoons ground cinnamon

1 teaspoon ground turmeric

2 teaspoons ground cumin

2 teaspoons ground coriander

1 large butternut squash, seeded and cut into large pieces

8 dried apricots halves

2½ cups gluten-free chicken broth

1 cup red quinoa

¾ cup crumbled feta cheese

salt and pepper (optional)

⅓ cup chopped fresh mint leaves, to garnish

1. Put the chopped onion into a blender with the tomato, ginger, and garlic. Process to a paste.

2. Heat the olive oil in a large saucepan or Dutch oven and cook the chicken over medium heat for 4–5 minutes, until browned all over. Remove from the pan and reserve.

3. Cook the sliced onion in the same pan over medium heat for 3–4 minutes. Stir in the spices and cook for an additional minute. Stir the garlic paste into the pan and cook for 2 minutes.

4. Return the chicken to the pan with the squash, apricots, and broth. Simmer for 15–20 minutes, until the chicken is cooked through. Season with salt and pepper, if using.

5. Meanwhile, cook the quinoa according to the package directions.

6. Divide the chicken mixture and quinoa among four serving plates and sprinkle with feta and mint to serve.

PER SERVING : 656 CALS | 21.6G FAT | 7.2G SAT FAT | 71.3G CARBS | 15.6G SUGAR | 10.9G FIBER | 48.5G PROTEIN | 880MG SODIUM

TURKEY, SESAME & GINGER NOODLES

TURKEY IS ONE OF THE LEANEST MEATS YOU CAN BUY AND IS AN INVALUABLE SOURCE OF PROTEIN. IT ALSO HAS A HIGH AMOUNT OF TRYPTOPHAN, WHICH CAN ACT AS A MOOD STABILIZER.

INGREDIENTS

5½ ounces egg noodles

1 tablespoon olive oil, for frying

2 garlic cloves, crushed

1¼-inch piece fresh ginger, peeled and diced

14 ounces turkey breast, cut into strips

2 cups snow peas

1½ cups broccoli florets

1 red bell pepper, seeded and sliced

2 scallions, trimmed and sliced

1½ cups bean sprouts

1 tablespoon sesame oil

1 tablespoon gluten-free soy sauce

1 tablespoon sweet chili sauce

juice of ½ lime

⅓ cup smooth, gluten-free peanut butter

⅔ cup roasted peanuts, chopped

⅓ cup fresh cilantro leaves, to garnish

1. Cook the egg noodles according to the package directions.

2. Heat the olive oil in a wok or large skillet and add the garlic, ginger, and turkey. Stir-fry over medium heat for 3–4 minutes, until the turkey is cooked through. Remove from the pan and reserve.

3. Add the snow peas, broccoli, and red pepper to the wok and stir-fry over medium heat for 4–5 minutes. Add the scallions and bean sprouts, and continue to cook for 1 minute.

4. Whisk the sesame oil, soy sauce, chili sauce, lime juice, and peanut butter together in a small bowl and add to the wok along with the turkey and noodles. Toss together really well.

5. Divide the turkey and noodles among four warm serving bowls and top with the peanuts and cilantro to serve.

This dish is delicious eaten hot or cold. You can take any leftovers to work the next day for an easy lunch.

PER SERVING : 675 CALS | 35.6G FAT | 6.2G SAT FAT | 50.2G CARBS | 11.5G SUGAR | 7.8G FIBER | 44.2G PROTEIN | 520MG SODIUM

PORK RAMEN NOODLE BOWL

THIS RECIPE GIVES YOU TWO HEARTY BOWLS OF SPICY SOUP—FULL OF FLAVOR AND NUTRIENTS TO POWER YOU THROUGH THE DAY.

INGREDIENTS

3½ cups chicken broth

½ red chile, seeded and sliced

½ green chile, seeded and sliced

1 garlic clove, peeled and sliced

1-inch piece fresh ginger, peeled and cut into strips

1 small carrot, peeled and cut into sticks

2 scallions, sliced

10½ ounces pork tenderloin, cut into strips

1 egg

4½ ounces egg noodles

1 bok choy, sliced

pepper (optional)

sesame seeds, to garnish (optional)

1. Put the broth into a large saucepan and bring to a simmer.

2. Add the red chile, green chile, garlic, ginger, carrot, and scallions and simmer for 2 minutes.

3. Add the pork and continue to simmer for 5 minutes.

4. Meanwhile, bring a small saucepan of water to a boil. Add the egg and cook for 5 minutes. Drain and peel when cool enough to handle, then halve lengthwise.

5. Add the egg noodles and bok choy to the pork mixture and cook for an additional 3–4 minutes.

6. Divide between two warm bowls and serve each portion with an egg half on top, sprinkled with pepper and sesame seeds, if using.

PER SERVING : 442 CALS | 15.7G FAT | 5.7G SAT FAT | 23.3G CARBS | 7.3G SUGAR | 4.3G FIBER | 43.8G PROTEIN | 1,800MG SODIUM

MEXICAN BEEF & BEAN BOWL

CHILI CON CARNE WITH EXTRA BEANS FOR PROTEIN AND FIBER, PLUS RED BELL PEPPERS FOR THEIR GREAT FLAVOR—PERFECT TO MAKE IN ADVANCE, BECAUSE THE FLAVORS IMPROVE OVER TIME.

INGREDIENTS

1 tablespoon olive oil

1 pound 2 ounces ground beef

1 onion, chopped

2 red bell peppers, seeded and sliced

2½ teaspoons chili powder

1½ cups drained and rinsed, canned red kidney bean

1½ cups drained and rinsed, canned cannellini beans

1⅔ cups canned diced tomatoes

1 tablespoon tomato paste

½ cup gluten-free vegetable broth

1 cup basmati or other long-grain rice

2 tablespoons chopped fresh cilantro

2 tablespoons sour cream

¼ teaspoon smoked paprika

salt and pepper (optional)

1. Heat the oil in a large skillet, add the beef, and cook for 2–3 minutes, until brown all over.

2. Add the onion and red bell peppers and cook, stirring occasionally, for 3–4 minutes.

3. Stir in the chili powder and cook for 1 minute, then add the kidney beans, cannellini beans, tomatoes, tomato paste, and broth. Bring to a simmer and simmer for 12–15 minutes. Season with salt and pepper, if using.

4. Meanwhile, cook the rice according to the package directions.

5. Stir the cilantro into the chili and serve in warm bowls with the rice, topped with a dollop of sour cream and a sprinkling of smoked paprika.

If you are vegetarian, you can omit the beef altogether and make your chili with beans and tomato sauce, adding plenty of spice and chopped herbs for extra flavor.

PER SERVING : 682 CALS | 25.4G FAT | 8.7G SAT FAT | 69.6G CARBS | 8.7G SUGAR | 11.3G FIBER | 37.9G PROTEIN | 200MG SODIUM

DESSERTS

CHOCOLATE GRANOLA WITH YOGURT

IF YOU LOVE CHOCOLATE, YOU WILL LOVE THIS RECIPE—CREAMY LEMON CURD YOGURT WITH FRESH BERRIES AND A HIT OF CHOCOLATE FROM THE FRESHLY MADE GRANOLA.

INGREDIENTS

½ cup coarsely chopped pecans

3 tablespoons pumpkin seeds

¼ cup slivered almonds

¼ cup dry unsweetened coconut

25 g/1 oz cacao nibs

¼ cup cashew nuts, coarsely chopped

¼ cup rolled oats

2 tablespoons unsweetened cocoa powder

1 tablespoon maple syrup

2 tablespoons lemon curd

¾ cup plain yogurt

1 cup hulled and halved strawberries

1 cup blueberries

¾ cup raspberries

⅔ cup blackberries

few mint leaves, torn

zest of 1 lemon

1. Put the pecans, pumpkin seeds, almonds, coconut, cacao nibs, cashew nuts, oats, cocoa powder, and maple syrup into a bowl and mix well together.

2. Stir the lemon curd through the yogurt.

3. Divide the fruit among four bowls, top with the lemon yogurt, then spoon the chocolate granola over the top. Sprinkle with mint leaves and lemon zest to serve.

If you like more "crunch" to your granola, spread the granola mixture on a baking sheet and bake in a preheated oven at 350°F for 12–15 minutes.

PER SERVING : 402 CALS | 26.6G FAT | 7.7G SAT FAT | 36.6G CARBS | 19.1G SUGAR | 9.9G FIBER | 10.9G PROTEIN | 40MG SODIUM

BLACKBERRY & APPLE CRISP

THIS DELICIOUS FRUITY DESSERT IS TOPPED WITH A NUTTY, OATY CRUMB TOPPING.
THE SWEET TASTE OF THE BLACKBERRIES IS BOOSTED BY THE APPLES AND ORANGE JUICE.

INGREDIENTS

1 cup rolled oats

⅔ cup all-purpose flour

½ cup pecans

½ cup walnuts

2½ tablespoons sesame seeds

⅓ cup firmly packed light brown sugar

½ cup coconut oil

2 large Granny Smith apples, peeled, cored, and thinly sliced

1⅓ cups blackberries

juice of 1 orange

2 tablespoons water

1½ tablespoons sugar

¼ cup skyr Icelandic-style yogurt

4 teaspoons maple syrup

2 tablespoons toasted slivered almonds, to serve

1. Preheat the oven to 350°F.

2. Put the oats, flour, pecans, walnuts, and sesame seeds into a food processor and process until they resemble coarse crumbs.

3. Add the brown sugar and coconut oil and process again.

4. Put the apples and blackberries into the bottom of a shallow ovenproof dish.

5. Sprinkle with the orange juice and water, followed by the sugar.

6. Spoon the crumb topping over the fruit, then bake in the preheated oven for 25–30 minutes, until the top is golden and the fruit is bubbling around the sides.

7. Put the skyr into a bowl and drizzle with the maple syrup. Gently run a spoon through the skyr to create a marbled effect.

8. Divide the crisp among four bowls and serve with a dollop of the skyr and a sprinkling of toasted slivered almonds.

Most skyr yogurt is not made with animal rennet. If you are unsure, however, and follow a vegetarian diet, you can replace the skyr with coconut yogurt.

PER SERVING : 834 CALS | 59.3G FAT | 27.1G SAT FAT | 81G CARBS | 43.8G SUGAR | 9.4G FIBER | 12.1G PROTEIN | TRACE SODIUM

QUINOA FRUIT SALAD

QUINOA IS A GRAIN THAT MAKES A GREAT CRUNCHY ADDITION TO A FRUIT SALAD.
ADDING MINT AND GINGER ALSO ADDS SOME SPICE.

INGREDIENTS

½ cup quinoa

1¾ cups water

2 teaspoons date nectar or honey (use date nectar for a vegan or raw option)

1 tablespoon dried cranberries

½-inch piece fresh ginger, grated

6–8 fresh mint leaves, finely chopped

⅓ cup hulled and halved strawberries

⅛ honeydew melon, peeled, seeded, and diced

1 nectarine, cut into wedges

½ cup blueberries

1 tablespoon toasted slivered almonds

1. Preheat the broiler to medium. Put the quinoa and water into a medium saucepan and bring to a boil, then reduce the heat and cook for 8 minutes. Drain well, then spread out over an aluminum foil-lined baking pan or broiler pan.

2. Drizzle with the nectar and toast the quinoa under the broiler for about 8 minutes, until it starts to turn golden.

3. Transfer the quinoa to a large bowl and stir in the cranberries, ginger, and mint.

4. Toss in the strawberries, melon, nectarine, and berries, then divide between two bowls, sprinkle with the almonds, and serve.

Use fruits of your choice in this fruit salad—pick those in season for freshness. If you are not vegan, it can be topped with a dollop of either yogurt or crème fraîche for a hint of creaminess.

PER SERVING : 280 CALS | 5.1G FAT | 0.5G SAT FAT | 53.8G CARBS | 23.1G SUGAR | 6.5G FIBER | 8.1G PROTEIN | TRACE SODIUM

RASPBERRY, CHIA SEED & PECAN DESSERTS

CHIA SEEDS MAY BE TINY, BUT THEY'RE PACKED WITH PROTEIN, FIBER, AND OMEGA-3 FATS. IN ADDITION TO THE HEALTH BOOST, THEY GIVE JUICES AND PUREED FRUITS GORGEOUS TEXTURE.

10 mins | 2 mins | 4

INGREDIENTS

3¼ cups raspberries

2 tablespoons chia seeds

1 mango, pitted, peeled, and chopped

1¾ cups Greek-style yogurt

3 kiwis, peeled and sliced

2 tablespoons pecans, toasted and coarsely chopped, to decorate

1. Put the raspberries into a food processor and process until smooth, then place in a bowl. Stir in the chia seeds and let stand—the chia seeds will gradually thicken the mixture to a preserve-like consistency.

2. Put the mango into a clean processor and process until smooth. Lightly stir through the yogurt, letting trails of the mango show through.

3. Layer the yogurt, raspberry-chia mixture, and kiwi slices in four glasses, finishing with yogurt on top.

4. Sprinkle the dessert with chopped pecans to serve.

Mango is 14 percent natural sugar, and this can be quickly converted into energy by the body. It is also rich in beta-carotene and vitamin C.

PER SERVING : 281 CALS | 10.8G FAT | 4.1G SAT FAT | 37.7G CARBS | 23.2G SUGAR | 11.8G FIBER | 12.8G PROTEIN | 40MG SODIUM

PUMPKIN PIE SMOOTHIE BOWL

PUMPKIN PIE IS NORMALLY FULL OF SUGAR WITH A PASTRY CRUST, BUT THIS LOVELY BOWL OF GOODNESS MAKES A FILLING DESSERT OR BREAKFAST.

INGREDIENTS

3½ cups, peeled, seeded, and chopped pumpkin or butternut squash

2 bananas, chopped

1 tablespoon coconut oil

½ tablespoon ground cinnamon

3 tablespoons maple syrup

1¾ cups Greek-style yogurt

3 tablespoons pumpkin seeds, toasted

2 tablespoons sesame seeds, toasted

¼ teaspoon freshly grated nutmeg

1. Put the pumpkin or squash into a saucepan with some water, bring to a boil, then simmer for 12–15 minutes, until tender.

2. Drain, return to the pan, and add the bananas, coconut oil, cinnamon, and maple syrup. Mash to a smooth consistency.

3. Divide among four bowls and top each one with a dollop of yogurt.

4. Sprinkle with the pumpkin seeds, sesame seeds, and nutmeg and serve hot or cold.

PER SERVING : 341 CALS | 14.8G FAT | 7.5G SAT FAT | 41.7G CARBS | 25.7G SUGAR | 3.3G FIBER | 15.7G PROTEIN | 40MG SODIUM

FRUIT & ALMOND MILK POWER BOWL

THE MUESLI SOAKS OVERNIGHT, WHICH HELPS TO START THE BREAKING-DOWN PROCESS AND MAKES IT EASIER TO DIGEST. IN-SEASON FRUIT WILL PROVIDE BETTER FLAVOR AND RICHER NUTRIENTS.

15 mins, plus soaking

None

4

1. Mix the oats, raisins, apricots, almonds, and apples together in a large bowl. Pour the almond milk over them and mix well. Let soak overnight.

2. Divide the muesli among four bowls and top each portion with a dollop of yogurt, some raspberries, strawberries, and blueberries, a drizzle of maple syrup, and a sprinkling of cacao nibs.

INGREDIENTS

3 cups rolled oats

⅓ cup raisins

8 dried apricot halves, chopped

⅔ cup slivered almonds

2 dessert apples, such as Gala or Golden Delicious, grated

2½ cups almond milk

¼ cup Greek-style yogurt

½ cup raspberries

⅓ cup hulled and sliced strawberries

⅓ cup blueberries

¼ cup maple syrup

2 tablespoons cacao nibs

For a quick version of this recipe, you could soak the muesli overnight, then just top with fresh fruit in the morning.

PER SERVING : 584 CALS | 17.7G FAT | 3.9G SAT FAT | 97.2G CARBS | 41.8G SUGAR | 14.4G FIBER | 14.8G PROTEIN | 80MG SODIUM

PINEAPPLE POWER CHEESECAKE BOWL

ADDING TOFU TO THE CREAM CHEESE INCREASES THE PROTEIN CONTENT AND GIVES THIS CHEESECAKE A HEALTHY BOOST!

15 mins, plus chilling
2 mins
4

INGREDIENTS

7 ounces tofu

¾ cup cream cheese

2 tablespoons maple syrup

grated zest of 1 orange

2 tablespoons pecans

½ fresh pineapple, peeled, cored, and chopped

2 tablespoons dry unsweetened coconut

2 teaspoons honey

8 sweet gluten-free oat cakes or rice cakes

1. Put the tofu, cream cheese, and maple syrup into a food processor and process until smooth.

2. Stir in the orange zest and divide the mixture among four small bowls. Chill in the refrigerator for 10 minutes.

3. Dry-fry the pecans, then coarsely chop.

4. Divide the pineapple among the bowls, then sprinkle with the chopped nuts and coconut.

5. Drizzle each bowl with a little honey.

6. Serve each portion with two sweet oat cakes or rice cakes.

The cheesecake base works for any fruit topping—try chopped strawberries and mint for a summer version, sprinkled with chopped dark chocolate for some decadence.

PER SERVING : 411 CALS | 27.6G FAT | 13.8G SAT FAT | 33.6G CARBS | 20G SUGAR | 3.7G FIBER | 9.3G PROTEIN | 280MG SODIUM

HEALTHY FRUIT & NUT BOWL

THIS FRUIT AND NUT BOWL IS A DELECTABLE SUGAR-FREE TREAT. THE CHIA SEEDS CREATE A PRESERVE-LIKE CONSISTENCY, MAKING EXCELLENT FRUIT DESSERTS.

15 mins, plus chilling

None

4

INGREDIENTS

1 orange

2 mangoes, peeled, pitted, and chopped

¼ cup chia seeds

¼–⅓ cup milk

2 tablespoons goji berries

seeds from 2 passion fruits

⅓ cup pineapple chunks

2 tablespoons sunflower seeds

2 tablespoons pumpkin seeds

⅓ cup red currants or blueberries

2 kiwis, peeled and sliced

2 tablespoons slivered almonds, toasted

1. Grate the orange and reserve the zest, then peel the orange and put the flesh into a food processor with the chopped mango. Process for a few seconds to break everything down.

2. Add the orange zest, chia seeds, and milk and process again for 20–30 seconds, scraping down any mixture from the side of the bowl. Let stand for 5 minutes.

3. Process the mixture again, then divide it among four bowls and chill in the refrigerator for 10 minutes.

4. Top with the remaining ingredients and serve.

This recipe has 4 tablespoons (¼ cup) chia seeds, to serve 4. Stick to this quantity as it is not recommended that you have more than 1 tablespoon of chia seeds a day.

PER SERVING : 294 CALS | 12G FAT | 1.3G SAT FAT | 44.6G CARBS | 29.9G SUGAR | 11.6G FIBER | 7.8G PROTEIN | TRACE SODIUM

STRAWBERRY & RHUBARB SMOOTHIE BOWL

HERE IS A DELICIOUS CREAMY SUMMER DESSERT—ROASTED RHUBARB SMOOTHIE TOPPED WITH STRAWBERRY PUREE AND SPRINKLED WITH FRESH FRUIT, NUTS, AND CACAO NIBS.

INGREDIENTS

2½ rhubarb stalks, cut into 1-inch pieces

1 teaspoon honey

¾ cup hulled strawberries

⅔ cup coconut yogurt

¾ cup coconut milk

1 tablespoon cacao nibs

1 tablespoon toasted slivered almonds

1 teaspoon chia seeds

1. Preheat the oven to 400°F.

2. Put the rhubarb into a roasting pan and drizzle with the honey. Roast in the preheated oven for 12 minutes, until soft. Let cool for 5 minutes.

3. Reserving two strawberries, put the remainder into a small blender, and blend to a puree.

4. Transfer the rhubarb to a blender or food processor with the yogurt and milk and process until smooth.

5. Divide the smoothie between two bowls. Swirl the strawberry puree through each serving. Slice the remaining strawberries and place on top, then sprinkle with the cacao nibs, almonds, and chia seeds.

If you don't have time to roast rhubarb, try a banana smoothie instead, using the same toppings, or even swap raspberries for the strawberry puree.

PER SERVING : 238 CALS | 16.5G FAT | 11.8G SAT FAT | 19.7G CARBS | 10.1G SUGAR | 4.7G FIBER | 4.1G PROTEIN | 40MG SODIUM

CRANBERRY & RASPBERRY SMOOTHIE BOWL

SMOOTHIE BOWLS ARE NOT ONLY GREAT FOR BREAKFAST, THEY ALSO MAKE PERFECT DESSERTS—LIGHT AND REFRESHING, BUT FULL OF FLAVOR.

INGREDIENTS

½ cup cranberries (frozen or fresh)

1⅔ cups raspberries

1 banana, sliced

1¾ cups almond milk

1 small peach, pitted and sliced into wedges

1 kiwi, peeled, halved, and sliced

1 tablespoon pomegranate seeds

1 tablespoon toasted slivered almonds

1. Put the cranberries, 1¼ cups of the raspberries, and the banana in a blender. Pour in the milk and process until smooth.

2. Pour into two bowls, top with the peach, kiwi, the remaining raspberries, the pomegranate seeds, and almonds, and serve.

Cranberries can be difficult to find all year round, but frozen ones are great in this—and they keep everything cool! You could also top with a few dried cranberries for added cranberry flavor.

PER SERVING : 223 CALS | 5.8G FAT | 0.2G SAT FAT | 42.5G CARBS | 22.1G SUGAR | 11.5G FIBER | 5.2G PROTEIN | 120MG SODIUM

NUTTY GRANOLA SUNDAES WITH YOGURT & MANGO

GRANOLA MAY BE MORE ASSOCIATED WITH BREAKFAST, BUT COMBINED WITH FRUIT AND YOGURT IT MAKES A REFRESHING DESSERT, OFFERING WELCOME ADDITIONAL TEXTURE AND CRUNCH.

10–15 mins

35–40 mins

INGREDIENTS

1 cup coarsely chopped almonds

⅔ cup coarsely chopped pecans

⅓ cup coarsely chopped cashew nuts

⅓ cup sunflower seeds

¾ cup pumpkin seeds

2 tablespoons sesame seeds

1⅓ cups rolled oats

3 tablespoons coconut oil

3 tablespoons maple syrup

2 teaspoons ground cinnamon

⅔ cup dried cranberries

½ cup Greek-style yogurt

1 mango, pitted, peeled, and chopped

1. Preheat the oven to 350°F.

2. Put the nuts into a large bowl with the seeds and oats, and mix well.

3. In a small saucepan, combine the coconut oil with the maple syrup and cinnamon over medium heat. When the coconut oil has melted, remove from the heat and stir into the nut mixture, mixing well.

4. Spread the mixture over a baking sheet and bake in the preheated oven for 30–35 minutes, shaking and stirring from time to time, until golden.

5. Let the granola cool before stirring in the cranberries.

6. Divide the granola among six bowls and serve layered with yogurt and chopped mango.

The choice of nuts and seeds is up to you, but a wide variety is always best to gain the most nutrients available.

PER SERVING : 646 CALS | 44.4G FAT | 10.9G SAT FAT | 52.6G CARBS | 25.9G SUGAR | 9.3G FIBER | 19G PROTEIN | TRACE SODIUM

MIXED FRUIT SOUP BOWL

THIS SUMMERY COLD FRUIT SOUP IS PERFECT FOR A HOT DAY,
AND IT IS RICH IN ANTIOXIDANTS DUE TO ITS BEAUTIFUL BRIGHT COLORS.

15 mins, plus chilling | None | 4

INGREDIENTS

2 papaya, peeled, seeded, and chopped

2 cups hulled strawberries

1 honeydew melon, seeded, peeled, and chopped

⅓ cup fresh mint leaves

1 tablespoon preserved ginger syrup

1 knob of preserved ginger

⅔ cup blueberries

1. Reserving 1 tablespoon of the chopped papaya, place the remainder in a food processor with 1¾ cups of the strawberries and process to a smooth puree.

2. Pour into a pitcher and chill in the refrigerator for 10 minutes.

3. Put all but 1 tablespoon of the chopped melon into the food processor with half the mint leaves, the ginger syrup, and preserved ginger. Process to a smooth puree. Pour into a pitcher and chill in the refrigerator for 10 minutes.

4. When you are ready to serve, divide each soup among four bowls, then use a knife to swirl them together. Drop a couple of ice cubes into each bowl.

5. Dice the reserved fruits and sprinkle them over the soup, together with the blueberries and the remaining mint leaves.

PER SERVING : 173 CALS | 0.9G FAT | 0.2G SAT FAT | 43.1G CARBS | 34.4G SUGAR | 5.7G FIBER | 2.2G PROTEIN | 0.1G SODIUM

AÇAI POWER BOWL

AÇAI BOWLS ARE A POPULAR CHOICE FOR BREAKFAST AND DESSERT. THIS METHOD IS A TIME-SAVING WAY TO MAKE DAIRY-FREE ICE-CREAM WITHOUT THE FUSS OF AN ICE CREAM MAKER.

8 mins, plus freezing | 8–10 mins | 4

INGREDIENTS

2 bananas, sliced

2½ cups raspberries

1 cup rolled oats

2 tablespoons dried cranberries

1 tablespoon sunflower seeds

3 tablespoons maple syrup

½ cup nondairy milk

1 tablespoon açai powder

⅔ cup blueberries

1. Place the banana slices and 1⅔ cups of the raspberries in a single layer on a cookie sheet and freeze for at least 2 hours.

2. Preheat a broiler to medium–hot. Mix the oats, cranberries, sunflower seeds, and maple syrup together and spread out over a baking sheet.

3. Cook under the preheated broiler for 8–10 minutes, turning frequently, until golden (watch the mixture carefully, because it can suddenly burn). Let cool.

4. Meanwhile, place half the frozen banana in a food processor with half the frozen raspberries and half the milk. Process until broken down. With the machine running slowly, add the açai powder and the remaining banana, raspberries, and milk, adding enough milk to produce an ice cream consistency.

5. Divide the ice-cream among four bowls, top with the blueberries, and sprinkle with the maple-toasted oats.

PER SERVING : 279 CALS | 4.5G FAT | 0.9G SAT FAT | 58G CARBS | 25.9G SUGAR | 10.1G FIBER | 5.6G PROTEIN | TRACE SODIUM

INDEX

This edition published by Parragon Books Ltd in 2018
and distributed by

Parragon Inc.
440 Park Avenue South, 13th Floor
New York, NY 10016
www.parragon.com/love-food

LOVE FOOD is an imprint of Parragon Books Ltd

ISBN 978-1-4748-8114-2

Printed in China

New recipes and introduction: Joy Skipper
New photography: Al Richardson
Editor: Emma Clegg

Additional images courtesy of iStock

NOTES FOR THE READER
This book uses standard kitchen measuring spoons
and cups. All spoon and cup measurements are level
unless otherwise indicated. Unless otherwise stated,
milk is assumed to be whole, eggs are large, individual
vegetables and fruits are medium, pepper is freshly
ground black pepper, and salt is table salt. A pinch of salt
is calculated as $1/16$ teaspoon. Unless otherwise stated, all
root vegetables should be peeled prior to using.

The times given are only an approximate guide.
Preparation times differ according to the techniques used
by different people and the cooking times may also vary
from those given.

Please note that any ingredients stated as being optional
are not included in the nutritional values provided. The
nutritional values given are approximate and provided as
only a guideline; they do not account for individual cooks,
measuring skills, and portion sizes. The nutritional values
provided are per serving or per item.

Vegetarians and vegans should be aware that some of
the store-bought ingredients used in the recipes in this
book might contain animal products. Always check the
packaging before use.